God created the cat so that man could caress the lion.

Fernand Mery

Vavra's Cats

Robert Vavra

William Morrow and Company, Inc.
New York

*For Penny and Bill, friends of all felines
and friends of mine.*

Copyright © 1986 by Robert Vavra

Library of Congress Cataloging-in-Publication Data

Vavra, Robert.
    Vavra's cats.

    1. Cats—Pictorial works.   2. Cats—Anecdotes.
3. Vavra, Robert.   I. Title.   II. Title: Cats.
SF446.V38   1986   636.8   86-12793
ISBN 0-688-05088-3

Printed in Switzerland

First Edition

1 2 3 4 5 6 7 8 9 10

Drawings by John Fulton

REFLECTIONS

SOME of the cats that stalk through my memory are Bagheera, the Three Little Kittens, Shere Khan, Felix, the tigers of Kumaon, the puma from the film *Sequoia,* and the leopard of Rudraprayag. If I shut my eyes and cast myself back through experience I can still hear, as I heard forty years ago in bed late at night, the roaring of the lions from Griffith Park Zoo haunting and far away, accompanied by the train whistle and distant rush of wheels over the same tracks that my friends and I crossed every Saturday, bicycling to see the big cats.

Fury was the only domestic cat I ever owned. Mine was a family whose pets were limited to other creatures. When I first saw him, I did not see a black kitten searching for scraps in the garbage behind Dale's Market. I saw Bagheera in miniature, "silent as a shadow and with a voice as soft as wild honey." If Kipling could not rouse hate in me for Shere Khan, he did make me love his black panther. Even though my mother tells of having had an

Angora cat that as a child she insists she adored, and though she allowed us to have snakes, alligators, lizards, a raccoon, rats, mice, guinea pigs, rabbits, Siamese fighting fish, hamsters, an owl, pigeons, doves, finches, a hawk, turtles, chickens, ducks, and our dog, Frisky, who lived to be twenty years old, still she said "no" when I begged her to allow Fury, as I named the black kitten, into the house. So my brother and I built a fortress of packing boxes in the front yard, large enough to house four small boys and a kitten.

Fury and I became inseparable; after-school hours were spent stretched out in our cardboard fortress with the sun beaming in through the opening of one of the boxes, bathing my face and half-closed eyes in golden warmth as the kitten slept on my chest while I dreamed of India and how Bagheera had rescued and decided Mowgli's acceptance into the pack.

"A black shadow dropped down into the circle. It was Bagheera the Black Panther, inky black all over, but with the panther markings showing up in certain lights like the pattern of watered silk. Everybody knew Bagheera, and nobody cared to cross his path; for he was as cunning as Tabaqui, as bold as the wild buffalo, and as reckless as the wounded elephant. But he had a voice as soft as wild honey dripping from a tree, and a skin softer than down.

"'O Akela, and ye the Free People,' he purred, 'I have no right in your assembly; but the Law of the Jungle says that if there is a doubt which is not a killing matter in regard to a new cub, the life of that cub may be bought at a price. And the Law does not say who may or may not pay that price. Am I right?'

"'Good! good!' said the young wolves, who are always hungry. 'Listen to Bagheera. The cub can be bought for a price. It is the Law.'

"'Knowing that I have no right to speak here, I ask your leave.'

(Continued on page 131)

In the beginning, when God created

the earth, both man and cat were

savage beasts who feared and

preyed on one another . . .

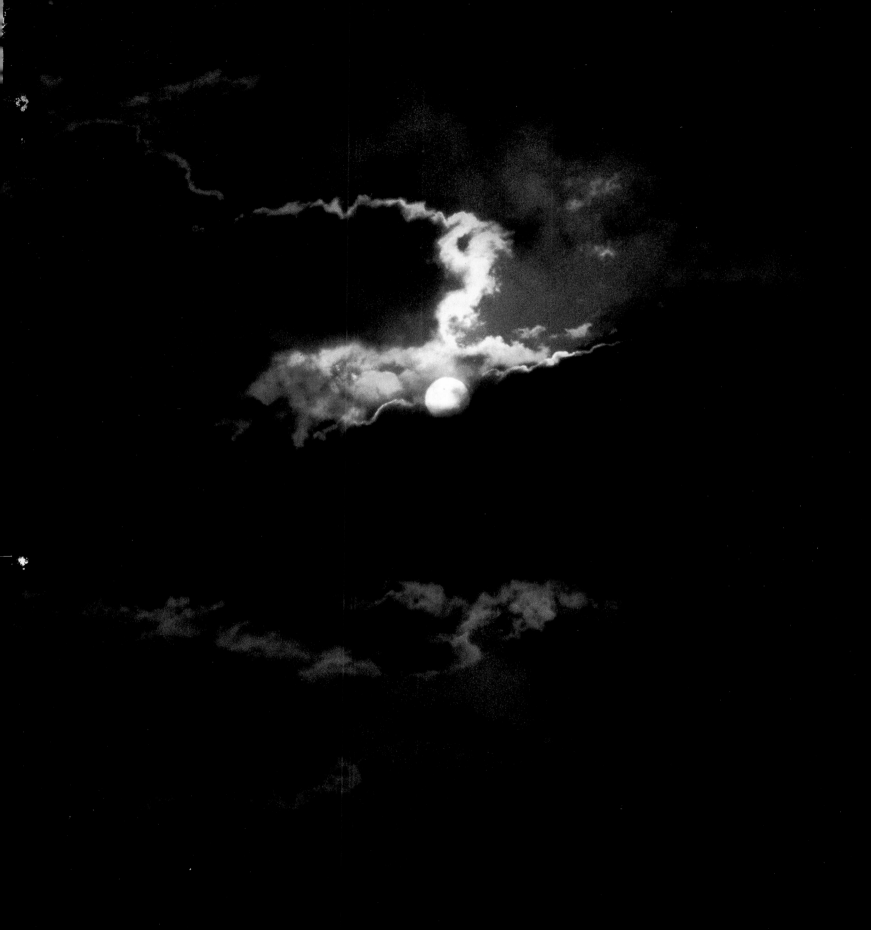

Now, Chill the Kite brings

home the night

    That Mang the Bat sets

free . . .

This is the hour of pride

and power,

    Talon and tush and claw

Oh, hear the call! Good

hunting all

    That keep the Jungle

Law!

        Rudyard Kipling

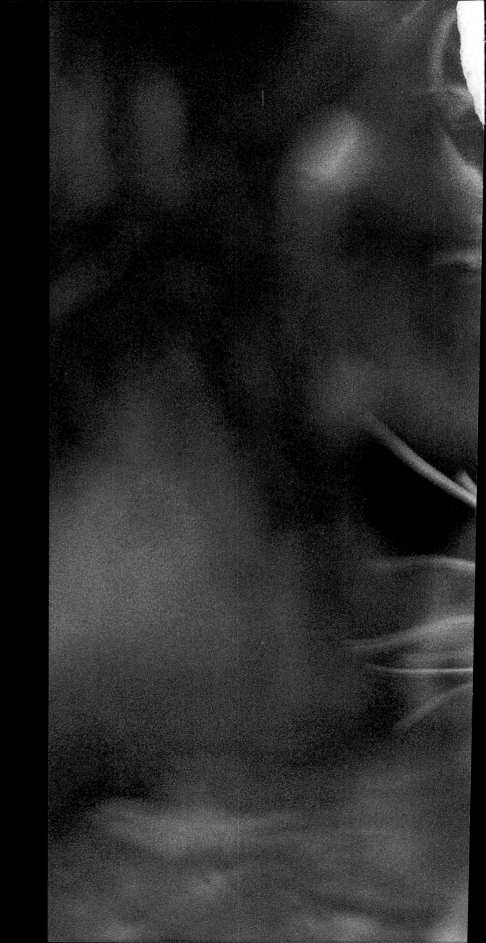

The same soft shivers ran through
all his body . . . the strain of the
long, vigilant watch, far from
smothering his joy, inflamed
it. . . . He waited in the shelter of
the branches . . . ready and strong
. . . for the leap that would kill his
prey.

Maurice Genevoix

I remember seeing the lion looking yellow and

heavy-headed and enormous. . . . He trotted . . .

big-footed . . . through the trees and toward the

tall grass and cover…

Ernest Hemingway

. . . they take the noble attitude

Of the great sphinxes that appear

to brood,

Stretched in the wastes, in dreams

that have no end;

Their loins are electric with fecundity,

And particles of gold, like finest

sand,

Stir vaguely their unfathomable eye.

Charles Baudelaire

Tiger! Tiger! burning bright

In the forests of the night,

What immortal hand or eye

Could frame thy fearful symmetry?

. . . Did he who made the Lamb

make thee?

William Blake

assage of time, man became

wild animal and more of a

eing, one capable of showing

and compassion not only to

nd but also to other creatures.

Only then did the cat feel secure enough to visit man's campfire and to purr under his caress. And so began an association that is unique among the creatures of this planet.

But with you, man, a cat converses; she coos

to you, looks into your eyes. . . . Towards

you she is no wild, solitary shadow . . .

because she has faith in you. A wild animal

is an animal which has no faith.

Domestication is simply a state of

confidence.

Karel Capek

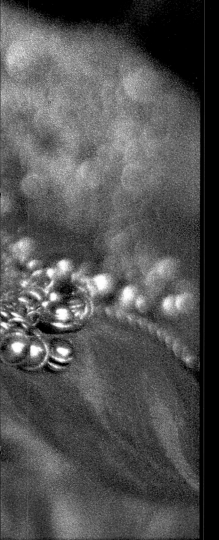

She spoke of Egypt, and a white

Temple, against night

She smiled with clicking teeth

and said

That the dead were never dead;

Said old emperors hung like bats . .

But empresses come back as cats!

William Rose Ben

My cat never laughs or cries he is always reasoning.

Unamuno

A kitten is in the animal

world what a rosebud is in

a garden.

Robert Southey

I am the cat who walks by himself

and all places are alike to me.

Rudyard Kipling

To respect the cat is the

beginning of the

aesthetic sense.

Anonymous

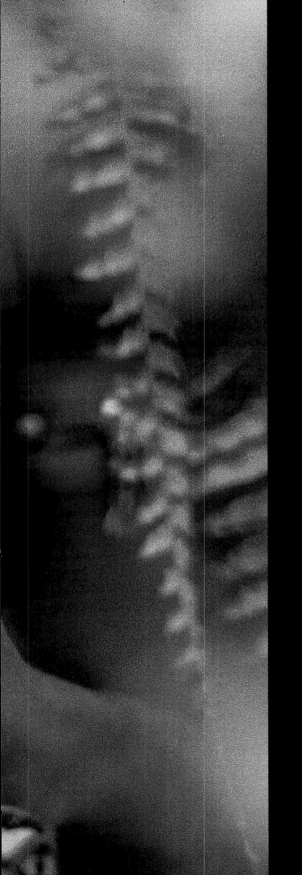

Of all the royal tribute—not the gold nor the ivory nor the diamonds and rubies—were as highly regarded by Tutankhamun as were these bright-eyed children of Bast.

Trajan Tenner

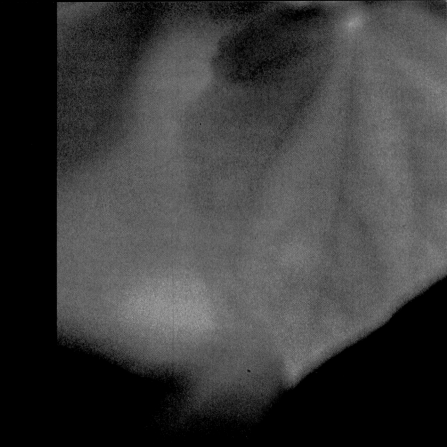

. . . he had a voice as soft as wild honey,

and a skin softer than down . . . as bold

as the wild buffalo and as reckless as the

wounded elephant . . . it was Bagheera

the Black Panther . . .

Rudyard Kipling

Her elegance and distinction gave

one an idea of aristocratic birth, and

among her own kind she must have

at least been a duchess.

Théophile Gautier

The serenity and majestic indifference, the padded paws and noiseless

step, the . . . eyes set in black fur with their grave regard
seemed to communicate calm and subdued agitation.

The Hon. Evan Charteris

Beloved cat! . . . my cat

of the garden, my cat of

the lilacs and the

butterflies.

Colette

The animal which the Egyptians

worshiped as divine, which the Romans

venerated as a symbol of liberty . . . has

displayed to all ages two closely blended

characteristics—courage and self

respect.

Saki

I like little kitty, her coat is so warm,

And if I don't hurt her she'll do me no

harm,

So I'll not pull her tail, nor drive her away,

But Kitty and I very gently will play.

Mother Goose (1839)

Wild beasts he created later,

Lions with their paws so furious;

In the image of the lion

Made he kittens small and curious.

Heinrich Heine

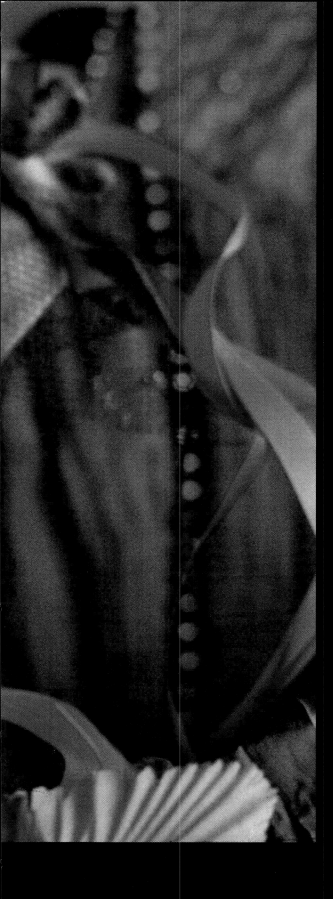

Caresses were agreeable to her, but she responded to them with great reserve, and only to those people whom her esteem favored, which was not easy to gain. She liked luxury, and it was always in the . . . furniture best calculated to show off her . . . beauty, that she was to be found.

Théophile Gautier

. . . *his face directly fronts your*

own; and then you meet your own

glance in the golden amber of his

widened round eye-stone

unexpectedly again, held fast like

an insect long ago extinct.

Rainer Maria Rilke

Before a cat will condescend

To treat you as a trusted friend

Some little token of esteem

Is needed, like a dish of cream;

And you might now and then supply

Some caviare, or Strassburg Pie,

Some potted grouse or

salmon paste—

He's sure to have his personal

taste.

T. S. Eliot

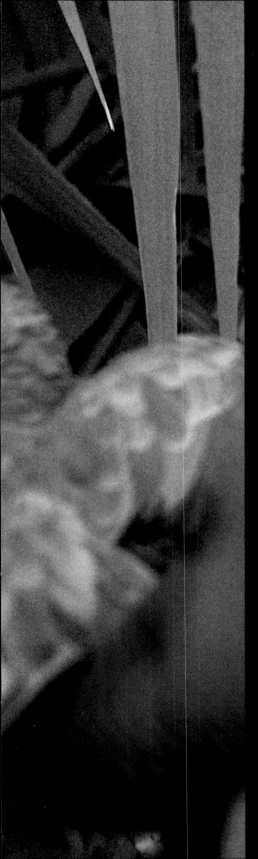

He was very fond of those delightful quiet,

mysteriously gentle animals . . . whose favorite

attitude is the prone pose of the sphinxes, which

seem to have passed their secrets to them.

Théophile Gautier

Gaze

With those bright languid segments . . . and

prick

Those velvet-ears—but pr'ythee do not stick

Thy latent talons in me—and upraise

Thy gentle mew—

John Keats

Tigers . . . red-gold . . . black-striped . . . serpent-like silence of movements and fateful stillness of lethe form . . . great strength of sinew . . . watchful orbs like two fiery gems set in a carved figure of rich stone. . . . Yet their hearts may also be conquered with kindness.

W. H. Hudson

Siamese . . . are the most human of all the

race of cats . . . For what disquieting blue eyes

stare out from the velvet masks of their faces!

Aldous Huxley

His function is to sit and be admired.

Georgina Strickland Gates

I love cats because they are so beautiful

aesthetically. They are like sculpture walking

around the house.

Wanda Toscanini Horowitz

His friendship is not easily won but

it is something worth having.

Michael Joseph

. . . indeed she was the very Venus

of cats for . . . grace and pose and

movement.

Edna Dean Proctor

Those deep-set eyes were

proud and suspicious,

completely masters of

themselves.

Colette

As Cleopatra lay in state

Faithful Bast at her side

did wait

Purring welcomes of soft

applause

Ever guarding with sharpened

claws.

Trajan Tennent

And gaze into your gazing

eyes,

   And wonder in a demi

dream

What mystery it is that lies

   Behind those slits that glare

and gleam . . .

Giles Lytton Strachey

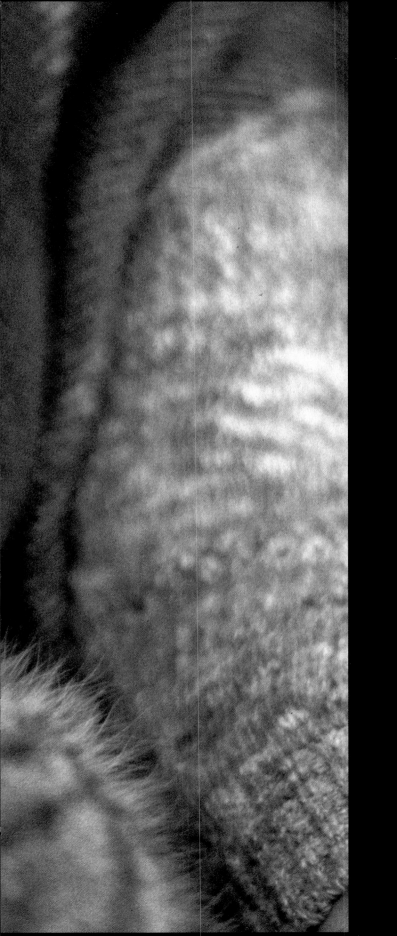

Who can believe that there is no soul

behind those luminous eyes.

Théophile Gautier

Cats are mysterious. . . . There is more passing in

their minds than we are aware.

Sir Walter Scott

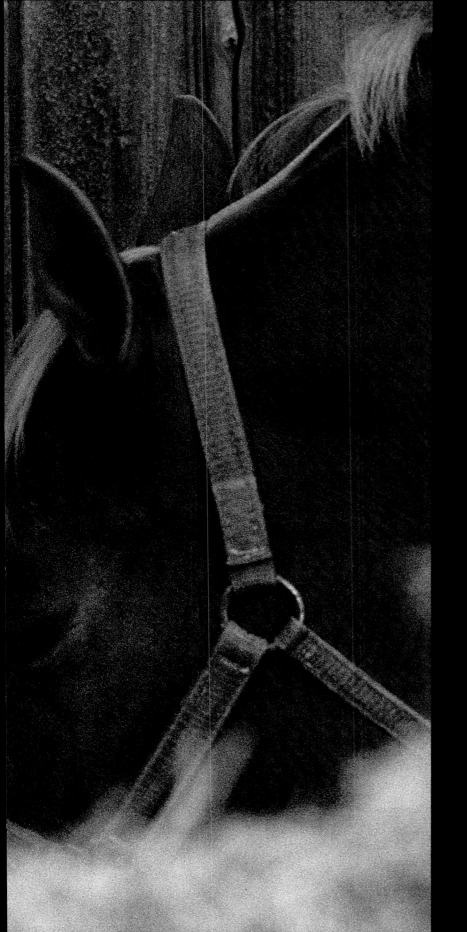

His amiable amber eyes

Are very friendly, very wise:

. . . grave and fat,

He sits regardless of applause,

And thinking . . .

What fun to be a cat!

Christopher Morley

. . . he stalked the carpets . . . like a

king and the ornate collar he always

wore added something more to his

presence.

James Herriot

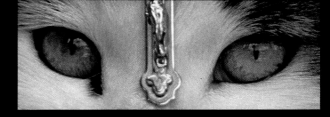

Ye my sisters, shall have no beast

but a cat.

Nunnery rule of the Middle Ages

Sullen . . . soft and bright

As the clouds of night,

Pays my reverent hand's caress

Back with friendlier gentleness.

You, a friend of loftier mind,

Answer friends alone in kind.

Just your foot upon my hand

Softly bids it understand.

Algernon Charles Swinburne

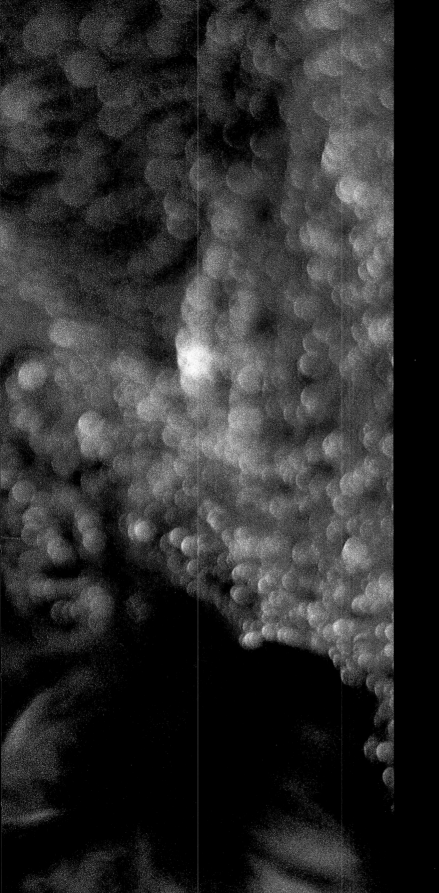

. . . his long vibrant whiskers . . . his

yellow eye, so ice-cold, so fire-hot . . .

gave him the deadly air of a

mousquetaire duelist. His soul was in

that eye . . . asking no favors and

granting no quarter.

Booth Tarkingt

I saw a proud mysterious cat,

I saw a cat 'twas but a dream,

Who scorned the slave that brought her

cream—

Unless the slave was dressed in style,

And knelt before her all the while…

Oh, what a proud mysterious cat.

Vachel Lindsay

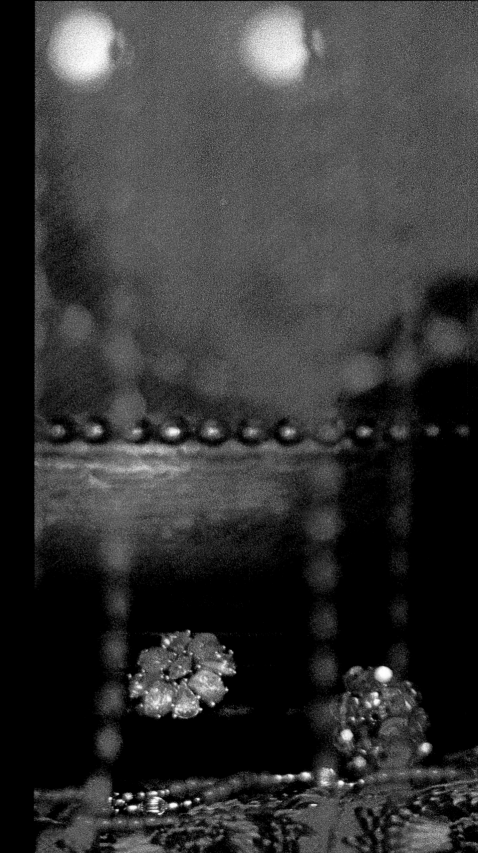

The blood of Bast flows in my veins,

And in my temple I was ritually fed.

My dish was carved of Lapis . . .

Agate, or Onyx…

Necklaces . . . adorned my throat.

Paul Gallico

It is a difficult matter to gain the

affection of a cat . . . He will be

friend, if he finds you worthy of

friendship, but not your slave.

Théop

Oh, fur-petaled purring

white chrysanthemum,

Your beauty could only be

eclipsed

By the face that launched a

thousand ships.

Trajan Tennent

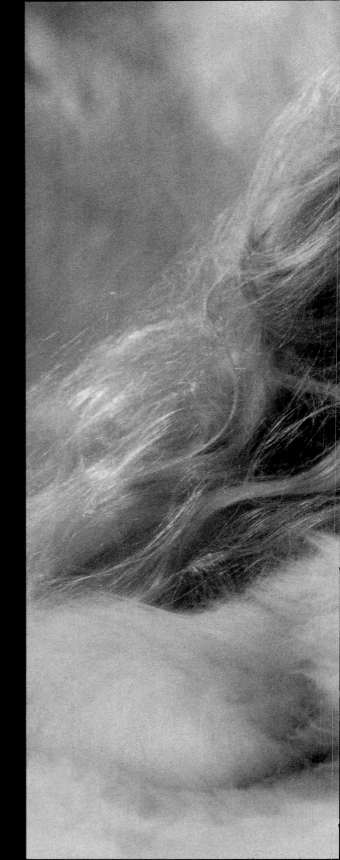

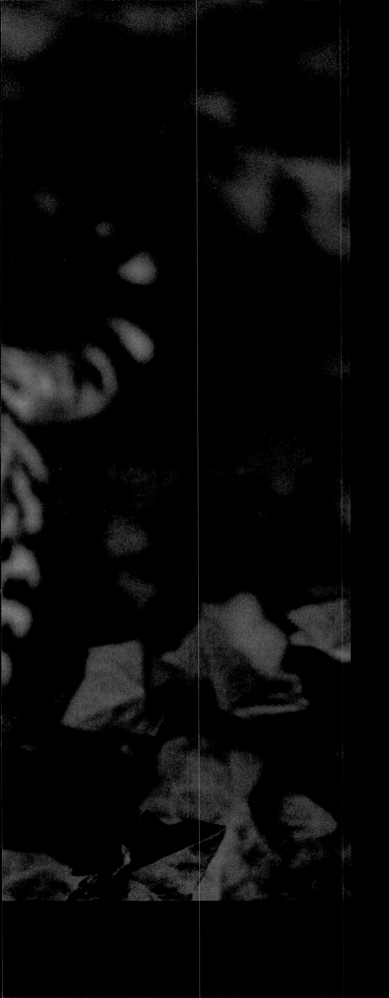

Except for the bright-plumaged birds, the cat surpasses all . . . the animal kingdom . . . in the variety of hues and . . . comes decorated with designs that Picasso might envy.

Paul Gallico

am a Cat.

am honorable.

have pride.

have dignity.
  Paul Gallico

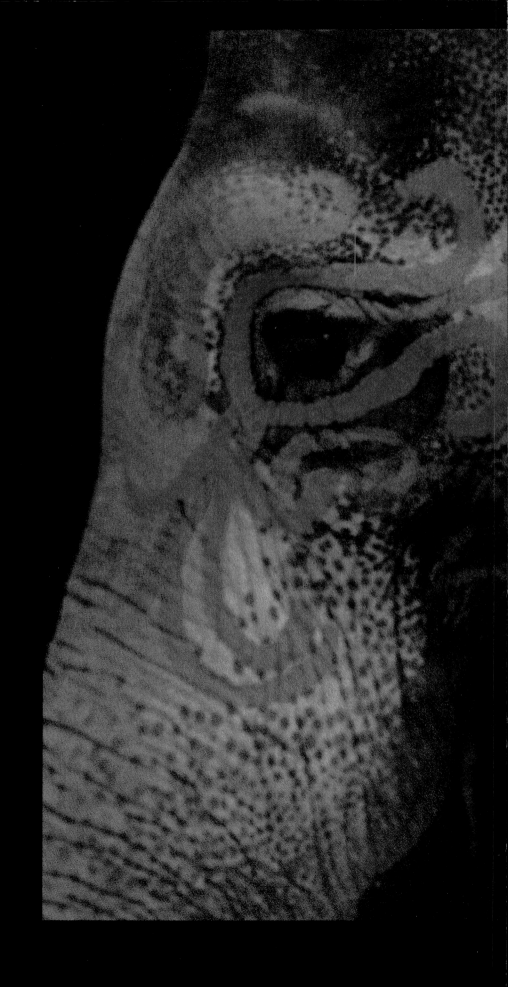

The smallest feline is a

masterpiece.

Leonardo da Vinci

Worshiped in state at Pharaoh's court . . .

From Thames to Nile, from gutter to throne,

Ever we hold our souls our own.

Comfort and penury, hopes and fears,

Are the toys of time and wreck of years,

But freedom the gift of eternity.

Sir Frederick Pollock

When I play with my cat, who knows

whether she is not amusing herself with

me more than I with her?

Michel de Montaigne

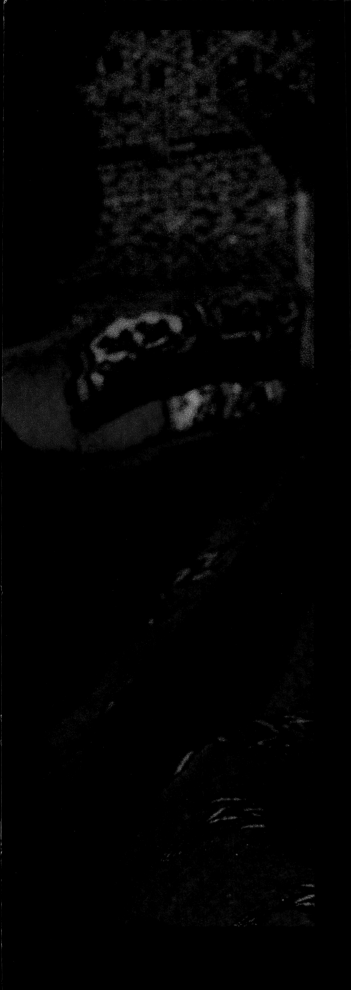

Praise be to thee, O Ra, exalted

Sekhem, thou art the Omnipotent

Cat, the avenger of the Gods . . .

Tomb wall inscription
XIX–XX Dynasties of Thebes

A kitten is more amusing than half the

people one is obliged to be with.

Lady Sydney Morgan

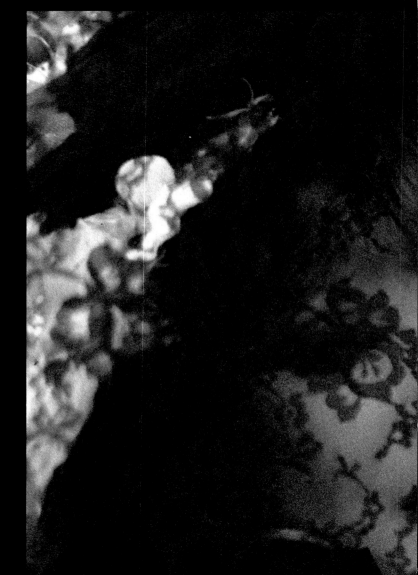

Our relationship was esoteric from the beginning. I was alone. She was alone. We united our solitude. We attained, between us, a definite sort of catification.

Kathleen Coyle

a cat poetry.

Jean Burden

It is, indeed, no small triumph to have combined the . . . liberty of primeval savagery with the luxury which only highly-developed civilization can command . . . to banquet on the dainties that wealth has bespoken for its table, and withal to be a free son of nature . . . a hunter. . . . This is the victory of the cat.

Saki

Klandaigi was the Cherokee name for the

puma kind, an honorable name. . . . But to

the puma Unaha Kanoos an even loftier title

had been given Koc Islito, the Cat of God.

Herbert Kavenel Sass

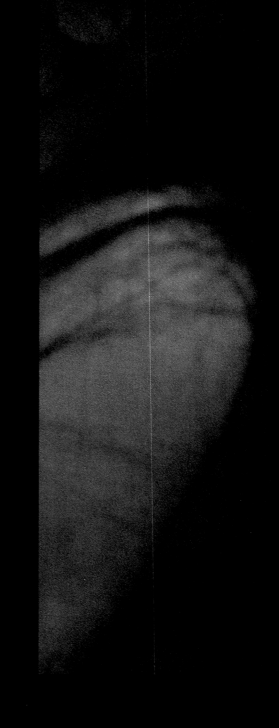

A house without a cat, and a well-fed,

well-petted, and properly revered cat, may

be a perfect house, but how can it prove

its title?

Mark Twain

Stately, kindly, lordly

friend

Condescend

Here to sit by me, and turn

Glorious eyes that smile and

burn.

Algernon Charles Swinburne

...ver leave me. . . .

...nything part us . . .

...cat and I am your

...ow and onwards into

...of peace.

Hilaire Belloc

Reflections, Continued, and a Comment on the Photographs

(Continued from page 6)

"'Speak then,' cried twenty voices.

"'To kill a naked cub is shame. Besides, he may make better sport for you when he is grown. Baloo has spoken in his behalf. Now to Baloo's word I will add one bull, and a fat one, newly killed, not half a mile from here, if he will accept the man's cub according to the Law. Is it difficult?'

"'There was a clamour of scores of voices, saying: 'What matter? He will die in the winter rains. He will scorch in the sun. What harm can a naked frog do us? Let him run with the Pack. Where is the bull, Bagheera? Let him be accepted.' And then came Akela's deep bay, crying: 'Look well—look well, O wolves!'

"Mowgli was still deeply interested in the pebbles, and he did not notice when the wolves came and looked at him one by one. At last they all went down the hill for the dead bull, and only Akela, Bagheera, Baloo, and Mowgli's own wolves were left. Shere Khan roared still in the night, for he was very angry that Mowgli had not been handed over to him.

"'Ay, roar well,' said Bagheera, under his whiskers, 'for the time comes when this naked thing will make thee roar to another tune, or I know nothing of man.'

"'It was well done,' said Akela. 'Men and their cubs are very wise. He may be a help in time.'

"'Truly, a help in time of need; for none can hope to lead the Pack for ever,' said Bagheera.

"Akela said nothing. He was thinking of the time that comes to every leader of every pack when his strength goes from him and he gets feebler and feebler, till at last he is killed by the wolves and a new leader comes up—to be killed in his turn.

"'Take him away,' he said to Father Wolf, 'and train him as befits one of the Free People.'

"And that is how Mowgli was entered into the Seeonee wolf-pack at the price of a bull. . . ."

Late every afternoon until I was called to dinner, I accompanied Fury as he played in the tall grass or stalked a butterfly or came bounding toward a twig lure that I dangled just out of his reach. Though it was impossible for me to realize it at the time, my small black companion was teaching me the basics of feline behavior as adeptly as if he had been a lion cub in the Ngorongoro Crater. He made me appreciate everything that is wonderful about cats, large and small. From him I actually learned timing and independence—lessons that one day would be invaluable in helping me make the most of the life I would choose. Fury also had the unique charm that is the passport of most kittens. Even the members of my family who admitted strong dislike for house cats were soon captivated by him and would cross the lawn to pluck him from his resting place on my chest, taking him in their arms and fawning over him. In fact, his cuteness was so seductive that I was certain by the first winter rains my parents, whose resistance had begun to be thawed by his charm, would soon allow my bedroom to become his.

However, winter did not have time to arrive. Fury's home was the fortress until summer passed and the leaves from the walnut tree were dropping onto the sagging cardboard boxes. We returned home one evening from the Roxy Theatre and seeing Victor Mature in *One Million B.C.*, rushing from the Model T Ford through the darkness to our own "saber-toothed panther," only to find that he had disappeared as mysteriously as he had arrived. So Fury was the first and last domestic-cat resident of 520 Burchett Street.

For some time after that my small boy's heart was heavy, as it seemed I, like Mowgli, had to return to the world of man, and my eyes teared each time I was brave enough to reread my hero's final departure from the jungle and his friends, ending with Bagheera's Farewell Song:

"'Listen, dearest of all to me,' said Baloo [the bear]. 'There is neither word nor will here to hold thee back. Look up! Who may question the Master of the Jungle? I saw thee playing among the white pebbles yonder when thou wast a little frog; and Bagheera, that bought thee for the price of a young bull newly killed, saw thee also. Of that Looking-over we two only remain; for Raksha, thy lair-mother, is dead with thy lair-father; the old Wolf-Pack is long since dead; thou knowest whither Shere Khan went, and Akela died among the dholes, where, but for thy wisdom and strength, the second Seeonee Pack would also have died. There remains nothing but old bones. It is no longer the Man-cub that asks leave of his Pack, but the Master of the Jungle that changes his trail. Who shall question Man in his ways?'

"'But Bagheera and the Bull that bought me,' said Mowgli. 'I would not—'

"His words were cut short by a roar and a crash in the thicket below, and Bagheera, light, strong, and terrible as always, stood before him.

"'Therefore,' he said, stretching out a dripping right paw, 'I did not come. It was a long hunt, but he lies dead in the bushes now—a bull in his second year—the Bull that frees thee, Little Brother. All debts are paid now. For the rest, my word is Baloo's word.' He licked Mowgli's foot. 'Remember, Bagheera loved thee,' he cried, and bounded away. At the foot of the hill he cried again long and loud, 'Good hunting on a new trail, Master of the Jungle! Remember, Bagheera loved thee.'

"'Thou hast heard,' said Baloo. 'There is no more. Go now; but first come to me. O wise Little Frog, come to me!'

"'It is hard to cast the skin,' said Kaa as Mowgli sobbed and sobbed, with his head on the blind bear's side and his arms round his neck, while Baloo tried feebly to lick his feet.

"'The stars are thin,' said Gray Brother, snuffing at the dawn wind. 'Where shall we lair today? for, from now, we follow new trails.'"

BAGHEERA

"In the cage my life began;
Well I know the worth of Man.
By the Broken Lock that freed—
Man-cub, 'ware the Man-cub's breed!
Scenting-dew or starlight pale,
Choose no tangled tree-cat trail.
Pack or council, hunt or den,
Cry no truce with Jackal-Men.
Feed them silence when they say:

132

'Come with us an easy way.'
Feed them silence when they seek
Help of thine to hurt the weak.
Make no *bandar*'s boast of skill;
Hold thy peace above the kill.
Let nor call nor song nor sign
Turn thee from thy hunting-line.
(Morning mist or twilight clear,
Serve him, Wardens of the Deer!)
*Wood and Water, Wind and Tree,
Jungle-Favour go with thee!*"

THE THREE

"On the trail that thou must tread
To the thresholds of our dread,
Where the Flower blossoms red;
Through the nights when thou shalt lie
Prisoned from our Mother-sky,
Hearing us, thy loves, go by;
In the dawns when thou shalt wake
To the toil thou canst not break,
Heartsick for the Jungle's sake:
Wood and Water, Wind and Tree,
Wisdom, Strength, and Courtesy,
Jungle-Favour go with thee!"

Fortunately there were other cats in the neighborhood, none of which we referred to by name,
only as "Miss Dix's cat" or "Mrs. McIntoche's cat."
But to me those local felines were only miniature
counterparts of those that crept through the pages
of Frank Buck's book or Martin and Osa Johnson's

book or whatever I was reading late at night in the top bed in the bunks I shared with my brother. What could have been more wonderful for a city boy who yearned for the jungle than the presence of sleek and mostly silent creatures who mirrored the behavior of rosette-spotted cousins in the Mato Grosso or black-and-orange-striped relatives in Kumaon. But the Burchett Street felines would rub against our legs, allow us to pat or chase them, and curl up on our laps.

The neighborhood cats fascinated me not only with their beauty and grace but also with their cunning. I had to try to keep one step ahead of them (as fifty years before in India my hero Jim Corbett had done with tigers and leopards) to prevent Mrs. McIntoche's cat from reaching the young mourning doves in their nest in the wisteria that draped violet over the front door, or to keep Miss Dix's cat from springing on top of the aviary at early evening to terrify the zebra finches. These dusk and nighttime experiences brought the hills or Kumaon and Rudraprayag into our backyard and I will be forever grateful to our spinster or widowed neighbor ladies for keeping what they felt were simply lap-warming tabbies but which in my imagination had no limits of size, craftiness, or magnificence.

I must admit that frequently their frightening screams and wails in the night caused me to slip deeper under the bedcovers. Actually it was not until I read Colette and learned those nocturnal cries most often expressed love and not hate or fear that I felt at all comfortable in the darkness with cat sounds.

"My thoughts turn to the house, to the fire and the lamp; there are books and cushions and a bunch of dahlias the colour of dark blood; in these short afternoons, when the early evenings turn the bay-window blue, decidedly it's time to be indoors. Already on the tops of the walls and on the still warm slates of the roofs, there appear with tails like plumes, wary ears, cautious paws and arrogant eyes, those new masters of our gardens, the cats.

"A long black tom keeps continual watch on the roof of the empty kennel; and the gentle night, blue with motionless mist that smells of kitchen gardens and the smoke of green wood, is peopled with little velvety phantoms. Claws lacerate the barks of trees, and a feline voice, low and hoarse, begins a thrilling lament that never ends.

"The Persian cat, draped like a feather boa along my window-sill, stretches and sings in honour of his mate dozing down below in front of the kitchen. He sings under his breath, as though in an aside, and seems to be awaking from a six months' sleep. He inhales the wind with little sniffs, his head thrown back, and the day is not far off when my house will lose its chief ornament, its two faithful and magnificent guests, my Angoras, silvery as the leaves of the hairy sage and the grey aspen, as the cobweb covered with dew or the budding flower of the willow.

"Already they refuse to eat from the same plate. While waiting for the periodical and inevitable delirium, each plays a part before the other, just for the pleasure of making themselves unrecognisable to each other.

"The male conceals his strength, walking with his loins low, so that the fluffy fringe of his flanks brushes the ground. The she-cat pretends to forget him, and when they are in the garden she no longer favours him with a single glance. In the house she becomes intolerant, and jealous of her prerogatives, grimacing with a look of bitter hatred if he hesitates to give way to her on the staircase. If he settles on the cushion that she wants, she explodes like a chestnut thrown on the fire, and scratches him in the face, like a true little cowardly female, going for his eyes and the tender velvet of his nose.

"The male accepets the harsh rules of the game and serves his sentence, as its duration is secretly fixed. Scratched and humiliated, he waits. Some days yet must pass, the sun must sink lower towards the horizon, the acacia must decide to shed, one by one, the fluttering gold of its oval coins. Then there must come some dry nights, and an east wind to frighten the last leafy fingers off the chestnut trees.

"Under a cold sickle of moon they will go off together, no longer a fraternal couple of sleeping and sparring partners, but passionate enemies transformed by love. He is compact of new cunning and bloodthirsty coquettishness, while she is all falsehood and tragic cries, equally ready for flight or for sly reprisals. The mysteriously appointed hour has but to sound and, old lovers and bored friends though they are, each will taste the intoxication of becoming for the other The Unknown."

Until I was a teenager, lions were my favorite

felines. How I loved them! For hours I would hang on the worn-smooth, dark pipe railing at the Griffith Park Zoo and stare into the yellowness of the eyes of those big African cats. Their penetrating gazes passed through me as though I didn't exist and stared beyond into an invisible vista. I would imagine herds of zebra and Mount Kilimanjaro rising in the background. Often I would glance back over my shoulder, attempting to find the target of their stares, but I saw nothing except the crowned cranes and egrets in the aquatic bird aviary.

Clyde Beatty's lion act was then the most exciting thing I had ever seen. Smells of sawdust and elephants blended with blasting circus music and the sight of Beatty leaping around the cage, firing his pistol and cracking his whip in that hurricane of roaring, snarling, growling, lunging, striking lions. The performance was magic to me. My small-boy's vision didn't see beyond the ring to the cramped cages, for I was completely caught up in a confrontation between courageous man and beautiful, dangerous beast. Clyde Beatty was for a time my hero and night after night I kept his books in bed with me:

"On January 13, 1932, I was giving my big cats a workout at the winter quarters of the Hagenbeck-Wallace Circus in Peru, Indiana. Nero, a big, powerful lion who had established himself as the arena boss, was about to go over a hurdle. Instead of making a clean jump he suddenly swerved in his course and came straight at me. It was one of those determined charges that an experienced trainer recognizes instantly. But though I knew it for what it was, I didn't have a chance to get set for it.

"The first thing I knew I was flat on my back on the floor of the arena with the lion standing over me. It was the worst moment I had ever known. And I haven't experienced one quite as bad since.

"As the big cat bent over me and bared the teeth with which he seemed about to mess up my features, I reached up with my right hand and planted it against his upper lip and nose. Then, with the strength born of desperation, I shoved him away from me, actually succeeding in working him back as far as my arm could reach. He gave his head a snap to release himself from my palm-hold, and as he did I found my hand in his mouth up to the wrist! This gave me a chance to gag him with my fingers. I needed that hand in my business and I was able to yank it out before he could recover his breath. The skin was scuffed where my hand and wrist had scraped against his teeth.

"Nero did not make for my face again, but seized what was nearest him. That happened to be the upper part of my leg. He grabbed it midway between the hip and the knee and tightened his jaw as if determined to snap the member in two. Having dug his teeth in deeply enough to satisfy himself (it developed later that they had sunk right into the bone), he began to drag me around the arena, bumping my head on the floor. Then he suddenly let me go, made for a nearby lioness and began licking her face with his tongue. The attack was over as fast as it had begun.

"What saved me from being torn to pieces was the fact that he happened to move in the direction of a lioness that was on his mind. He had forgotten her momentarily in his determination to get me, but now that he was near her again he remembered that she was his main concern. The attendants outside the cage, frantically working their poles and yelling in an effort to distract the beast, had little effect on him. There was nothing else they could do. It would have amounted to suicide to enter the ring and try to fight him off.

"It is my belief that the animal's attack on me was related to my having been standing near the female that had captured his interest. She was in heat and her presence excited him. In a situation of this kind an animal is capable of honest-to-goodness jealousy. If I had been another male lion, Nero could not have regarded my presence more suspiciously."

From the feline adventures that came to me via our Brand Public Library, one that is still etched on my mind is David Livingstone's account of being attacked by a lion; and thereafter each time I saw Miss Dix's tabby shaking a still-alive gopher, our spinster neighbor's neatly manicured front lawn became in my imagination the grass of the African veldt:

"It is well known that if one in a troop of lions is killed the others take the hint and leave that part of the country. So the next time the herds were attacked, I went with the people, in order to encourage them to rid themselves of the annoyance by destroying one of the marauders. We found the lions on a small hill about a quarter of a mile in length, and covered with trees. A circle of men was formed round it, and they gradually closed up, ascending pretty near to each other. Being down below on the plain with a native schoolmaster, named Mebalwe, a most excellent man, I saw one of the lions sitting on a piece of rock within the now closed circle of men. Mebalwe fired at him before I could, and the ball struck the rock on which the animal was sitting. He bit at the spot struck, as a dog does at a stick or stone thrown at him; then leaping away, broke through the opening circle and escaped unhurt. The men were afraid to attack him, perhaps on account of their belief in witchcraft. When the circle was re-formed, we saw two other lions in it; but we were afraid to fire lest we should strike the men, and they allowed the beasts to burst through also.

"If the Bakatla had acted according to the custom of the country, they would have speared the lions in their attempt to get out. Seeing we could not get them to kill one of the lions, we bent our footsteps towards the village; in going round the end of the hill, however, I saw one of the beasts sitting on a piece of rock as before, but this time he had a little bush in front. Being about thirty yards off, I took good aim at his body through the bush, and fired both barrels into it. The men then called out, "He is shot, he is shot!" Others cried, "He has been shot by another man too; let us go to him!" I did not see any one else shoot at him, but I saw the lion's tail erected in anger behind the bush, and, turning to the people, 137 said, "Stop a little till I load again." When in the act of ramming down the bullets I heard a shout. Starting, and looking half round, I saw the lion just in the act of springing upon me. I was upon a little height: he caught my shoulder as he sprang, and we both came to the ground below together. Growling horribly close to my ear, he shook me as a terrier dog does a rat. The shock produced a stupor similar to that which seems to be felt by a mouse after the first shake of a cat. It caused a sort of dreaminess, in which there was no sense of pain nor feeling of terror, though quite conscious of all that was happening. It was like what patients partially under the influence of chloroform describe, who see all the operation, but feel not the knife. This singular condition was not the result of any mental process. The shake annihilated fear, and allowed no sense of horror in looking round at the beast. This peculiar state is probably produced in all animals killed by the carnivora; and if so, is a merciful provision by our benevolent Creator for lessening the pain of death.

"Turning round to relieve myself of the weight, as he had one paw on the back of my head, I saw his eyes directed to Mebalwe, who was trying to shoot him at a distance of ten or fifteen yards. His gun, a flint one, missed fire in both barrels; the lion immediately left me, and attacking Mebalwe, bit his thigh. Another man, whose life I had saved before, after he had been tossed by a buffalo, attempted to spear the lion while he was biting Mebalwe. He left Mebalwe and caught this man by the shoulder, and he fell down dead. The whole was the work of a few moments, and must have been his paroxysm of dying rage. In order to take out the charm from him, the Bakatla on the following day made a huge bonfire over the carcase, which was declared to be that of the largest lion they had ever seen."

I can't remember at what age I discovered Jim Corbett's books, but what I do know is that I have since reread them more times than any other books in my library. From no other human, except my father, have I gained so much knowledge about the ways of nature. From him I learned to track through sight, sound, and smell—lessons that would later be of immense help in my behavioral studies of wild equines in France and of fighting bulls in Spain. To me his involvement with the jungle was awe-inspiring—to him it was both an obsession and elementary to his survival. Jim Corbett spent countless nights alone there, armed only with a single-shot rifle (this was India seventy years ago). Often he was the hunted and not the hunter, stalked in the moonless blackness by the Champawat man-eating tiger that claimed more than 438 human victims before being stopped by Corbett in 1911, or by the marauding leopard of Rudraprayag that brought tragedy to the families of 125 men, women, and children. However, most of Corbett's experiences with big cats were not spent with these abnormal animals that through injury or old age were forced to change their diet from the more difficult to catch four-legged hoofed

138

creatures of the jungle to the slower, not as alert, two-legged easy prey who inhabited villages on the edge of the forest.

Of all the creatures of the Indian forest, Corbett most loved tigers, and he probably knew more about them and their ways than any human being then or since. He writes: "Those of us who lack the opportunity of forming our own opinion on any particular subject are apt to accept the opinions of others, and in no case is this more apparent than in the case of tigers—here I do not refer to man-eaters in particular, but to tigers in general. The author who first used the words 'as cruel as a tiger' and 'as bloodthirsty as a tiger,' when attempting to emphasize the evil character of the villain of his piece, not only showed a lamentable ignorance of the animal he defamed, but coined phrases which have come into universal circulation, and which are mainly responsible for the wrong opinion of tigers held by all except that very small proportion of the public who have the opportunity of forming their own opinions.

"When I see the expression 'as cruel as a tiger' and 'as bloodthirsty as a tiger' in print, I think of a small boy armed with an old muzzle loading gun—the right barrel of which was split for six inches of its length, and the stock and barrels of which were kept from falling apart by lashings of brass wire—wandering through the jungles of the terai and *bhabar* in the days when there were ten tigers to every one that now survives; sleeping anywhere he happened to be when night came on, with a small fire to give him company and warmth, wakened at intervals by the calling of tigers, sometimes in the distance, at other times near at hand; throwing another stick on the fire and turning over and continuing his interrupted sleep without one thought of unease; knowing that from his own short experience and from what others, who like himself had spent their days in the jungles, had told him, that a tiger, unless molested, would do him no harm; or during the daylight hours, avoiding any tiger he saw, and when that was not possible, standing perfectly still until it had passed and gone, before continuing on his way. And I think of him on one occasion stalking half-a-dozen jungle fowl that were feeding in the open, and on creeping up to a plum bush and standing up to peer over, the bush heaving and a tiger walking out on the far side and, on clearing the bush, turning round and looking at the boy with an expression on its face which said as clearly as any words, 'Hello, kid, what the hell are you doing here?' and, receiving no answer, turning round and walking away very slowly without once looking back. And then again I think of the tens of thousands of men, women and children who, while working in the forest or cutting grass or collecting dry sticks, pass day after day close to where tigers are lying up and who, when they return safely to their homes, do not even know that they have been under the observation of this so-called 'cruel and bloodthirsty' animal.

"Half a century has rolled by since the day the

tiger walked out of the plum bush, the latter thirty-two years of which have been spent in the more or less 'regular pursuit of man-eaters,' and though sights have been seen which would have caused a stone to weep, I have not seen a case where a tiger has been deliberately cruel or when it has been blood-thirsty to the extent that it has killed, without provocation, more than it has needed to satisfy its hunger or the hunger of its cubs.''

"A tiger's function in the scheme of things is to help maintain the balance in nature and if, on rare occasions when driven by dire necessity, he kills a human being or when his natural food has been ruthlessly exterminated by man he kills two per cent of the cattle he is alleged to have killed, it is not fair that for these acts a whole species should be branded as being cruel and blood-thirsty.''

That Jim Corbett did carry a rifle and did kill tigers and leopards might cause some modern environmentalists to shudder. However, to the persons who lived in the villages that were prowled by one of the man-eaters of Kumaon, this slightly built, modest British naturalist was a savior. Perhaps one of the fascinating things about the domestic cat is its primordial side. On one hand, they can be our trusted friends and affectionate companions, and on the other, they, like their larger cousins, are the most effective of nature's predators. We can love cats, admire them, respect them, be awed by their beauty, and yet we can be fascinated by their mystery and intrigued by the terror that they can inspire. On the subject of feline-inspired terror, Corbett writes of the leopard of Rudraprayag:

"The word 'terror' is so generally and universally used in connexion with everyday trivial matters that it often fails to convey, when intended to do so, its real meaning. I should like, therefore, to give you some idea of what terror—real terror—meant to the 50,000 inhabitants living in the 500 square miles of Garhwal in which the man-eater was operating, and to the 60,000 pilgrims who annually passed through that area, between the years 1918 and 1926. And I shall give a few instances to show you what grounds the inhabitants, and the pilgrims, had for that terror.

"No curfew order has ever been more strictly enforced or more implicitly obeyed than the curfew imposed by the Man-Eating Leopard of Rudraprayag.

"During the normal hours of sunlight, life in that area carried on in a normal way. Men went long distances to the bazaars to transact business, or to outlying villages to visit relatives or friends. Women went up the mountainsides to cut grass for thatching or for cattle fodder. Children went to school or into the jungles to graze goats or to collect dry sticks. And, if it was summer, pilgrims either singly or in large numbers toiled along the pilgrim routes on their way to, or from, the sacred shrines of Kedarnath and Badrinath.

"As the sun approached the western horizon and the shadows lengthened, the behaviour of the

entire population of the area underwent a very sudden and a very noticeable change. Men who had sauntered to the bazaar or to outlying villages were hurrying home; women carrying great bundles of grass were stumbling down the steep mountainsides; children who had loitered on their way from school, or who were late in bringing in their flocks of goats or the dry sticks they had been sent out to collect, were being called by anxious mothers; and the weary pilgrims were being urged by any local inhabitant who passed them to hurry to shelter.

"When night came an ominous silence brooded over the whole area: no movement, no sound anywhere. The entire local population was behind fast-closed doors—in many cases, for further protection, with additional doors to the existing outer ones—and those pilgrims who had not been fortunate enough to find accommodation in houses were huddled close together in pilgrim shelter. Whether in house or in shelter all were silent, for fear of attracting the dreaded man-eater.

"This is what terror meant to the people of Garhwal, and to the pilgrims, for eight long years."

Corbett then offers five or six first-person accounts of encounters with the leopard, one of which will suffice here:

"A neighbour had dropped in to spend the period of a long smoke with a friend. The room was L-shaped and the only door in it was not visible from where the two men sat on the floor smoking, with their backs to the wall. The door was shut but not fastened, for up to that night there had been no human kills in the village.

"The room was in darkness and the owner of it had just passed the *hookah* (Indian pipe with a large clay bowl varying in diameter from four to six inches) to his friend when the *hookah* fell to the ground, scattering a shower of burning charcoal and tobacco. Telling his friend to be more careful or he would set on fire the blanket on which they were sitting, as well as their clothes, the man bent forward to gather up the burning embers, and as he did so, the door came into view. A young moon was near setting, and silhouetted against it the man saw a leopard carrying his friend through the door.

"When recounting the incident to me a few days later the man said, 'I am speaking the truth, Sahib, when I tell you I never heard even so much as the intake of a breath, or any other sound, from my friend who was sitting only an arm's length from me, either when the leopard was killing him, or when it was carrying him away. There was nothing I could do for my friend, so I waited until the leopard had been gone some little while, and then I crept up to the door and hastily shut and secured it.'"

In Chapter 22 of his book, Jim Corbett describes one of his own nights of terror with the leopard:

"Accompanied by Madho Singh and one of the villagers to show me the way, I went down to the kill. The cow had been killed in a deep ravine

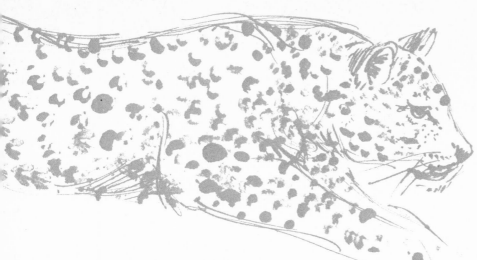

a quarter of a mile from the road and a hundred yards from the river. On one side of the ravine there were big rocks with dense brushwood between, and on the other side a few small trees, none of which was big enough to sit in. Under the trees and about thirty yards from the kill there was a rock with a little hollow at the base of it. In this hollow I decided to sit.

"Both Madho Singh and the villager objected very strongly to my sitting on the ground, but as this was the first animal kill I had got since my arrival at Rudraprayag, in a place where it was reasonable to expect the leopard to come at an early hour—about sundown—I overruled their objections and sent them back to the village.

"My seat was dry and comfortable, and with my back to the rock and a small bush to conceal my legs I was confident the leopard would not see me and that I should be able to kill it before it was aware of my presence. I had provided myself with a torch and a knife, and with my good rifle across my knees I felt that in this secluded quiet spot my chances of killing the leopard were better than any I had yet had.

"Without movement and with my eyes on the rocks in front of me I sat through the evening, each second bringing the time nearer when the undisturbed and unsuspecting leopard would of a certainty return to his kill. The time I had been waiting for had come, and was passing. Objects near at hand were beginning to get blurred and indistinct. The leopard was a little later in coming than I had expected him to be, but that was not worrying me. I had a torch, the kill was only thirty yards from me, and I would be careful over my shot and make quite sure that I did not have a wounded animal to deal with.

"In the deep ravine there was absolute silence. The hot sun of the past few days had made the dead leaves on the bank on which I was sitting as dry as tinder; this was very reassuring, for it was now dark and, whereas previously I had depended on my eyes for protection, I now had to depend on my ears. With thumb on the button of the torch and finger on trigger, I was prepared to shoot in any direction in which I heard the slightest sound.

"The failure of the leopard to appear was beginning to cause me uneasiness. Was it possible that from some concealed place among the rocks he had been watching me all these hours, and was he now licking his lips in anticipation of burying his teeth in my throat?—for he had long been deprived of human flesh. In no other way could I account for his not having come, and if I were to have the good fortune to leave the ravine on my feet, my ears would have to serve me now as they had never served me before.

"For what seemed like hours I strained my ears, and then, noticing it was getting darker than it should have been, I looked up and saw that a heavy bank of clouds was drifting across the sky, obscuring the stars one by one. Shortly thereafter big drops of rain started to fall and, where there had been absolute and complete silence, there was now sound and movement all round—the opportunity the leopard had been waiting for had come.

Hastily taking off my coat, I wound it round my neck, fastening it securely in place with the sleeves. The rifle was now useless but might help to cause a diversion; so transferring it to my left hand I unsheathed my knife and got a good grip on it with my right hand. The knife was what is called an Afridi stabbing knife, and I devoutly hoped it would serve me as well as it had served its late owner. When I bought it from the government store at Hangu on the North-west Frontier, the Deputy Commissioner had drawn my attention to a label attached to it and to three notches on the handle, and said it had figured in three murders. Admittedly a gruesome relic, but I was glad to have it in my hand, and I clutched it tight while the rain lashed down.

"Leopards, that is, ordinary forest leopards, do not like rain and invariably seek shelter, but the man-eater was not an ordinary leopard, and there was no knowing what his likes or dislikes were, or what he might or might not do.

"When Madho Singh was leaving, he asked how long I intended to sit up, and I had answered, 'Until I have shot the leopard.' I could now expect no help from him, and of help I was at that time in urgent need. Should I go or should I remain, were the questions that were exercising me, and the one was as unattractive as the other. If the leopard up to then had not seen me, it would be foolish to give my position away and possibly fall across him on the difficult ground I would have to negotiate on my way up to the pilgrim road. On the other hand, to remain where I was for another six hours—momentarily expecting to have to fight for my life with an unfamiliar weapon—would put a strain on my nerves that they were not capable of standing. Getting to my feet and shouldering the rifle, I set off.

"I had not far to go, only about 500 yards, half of which was over wet clay and the other half over rocks worn smooth with bare feet and the hooves of cattle. Afraid to use the torch for fear of attracting the man-eater, and with one hand occupied with the rifle and the other with the knife, my body made as many contacts with the ground as my rubber-shod feet. When I eventually reached the road I sent a full-throated *cooee* into the night, and a moment later I saw a door in the village far up the hillside open and Madho Singh and his companion emerge, carrying a lantern.

"When the two men joined me, Madho Singh said he had had no uneasiness about me until the rain started, and that he had then lit the lantern and sat with his ear against the door, listening. Both men were willing to accompany me back to Rudraprayag, so we set out on our seven-mile walk, Bachi Singh leading, Madho Singh carrying the lantern following, and I bringing up the rear. When I returned next day I found the kill had not been touched, and on the road I found the tracks of the man-eater. What time had elapsed between our going down the road and the man-eater's following us, it was not possible to say.

"When I look back on that night, I look back on it as my night of terror. I have been frightened times without number, but never have I been frightened as I was that night, when the unexpected rain came down and robbed me of all my defences and left me for protection only a murderer's knife.''

After finishing his story of having dispatched the man-eating leopard of Rudraprayag in 1926, Jim Corbett's sensitivity to and compassion for humans as well as animals radiates in his book's epilogue:

"The events I have narrated took place in 1925–6. Sixteen years later, that is, in 1942, I was doing a war job in Meerut and my sister and I were invited one day by Colonel Flye to help entertain wounded men at a garden party. The men, some fifty or sixty in number, and from all parts of India, were sitting round a tennis court and were just finishing a very sumptuous tea and getting to the smoking stage, when we arrived. Taking opposite sides of the court, my sister and I started to go round the circle.

"The men were all from the Middle East and, after a rest, were to be sent to their homes, some on leave, and some on discharge.

"Music, in the form of a gramophone with Indian records, had been provided by Mrs. Flye, and as my sister and I had been requested to stay until the party was over—which would be in about two hours' time—we had ample time to make our circuit of the wounded men.

"I had got about halfway round the circle when I came to a boy sitting in a low chair; he had been grievously wounded, and on the ground near his chair were two crutches. At my approach he very painfully slid off his chair and attempted to put his head on my feet. He was woefully light, for he had spent many months in the hospital, and when I had picked him up and made him comfortable in his chair, he said, 'I have been talking with your lady sister, and when I told her I was a Garhwali, she told me who you were. I was a small boy when you shot the man-eater, and as our village is far from Rudraprayag I was not able to walk there, and my father not being strong was unable to carry me, so I had to stay at home. When my father returned he told me he had seen the man-eater, and that with his own eyes he had seen the Sahib who had shot it. He also told me of the sweets that had been distributed that day—his share of which he had brought back for me—and of the great crowds he had seen. And now, Sahib, I will go back to my home with great joy in my heart, for I shall be able to tell my father that with my own eyes I have seen you, and maybe, if I can get any one to carry me to the *Mela* that is annually held at Rudraprayag to commemorate the death of the man-eater, I shall tell all the people there that I have seen and had speech with you.'

"A cripple, on the threshold of manhood, returning from the wars with a broken body, with no thought of telling of brave deeds done, but only eager to tell his father that with his own eyes he had seen the man who years ago he had not had the opportunity of seeing, a man whose only claim to remembrance was that he had fired one accurate shot.

"A typical son of Garhwal, of that simple and

hardy hill folk; and of that greater India, whose sons only those few who live among them are privileged to know, It is these big-hearted sons of the soil, no matter what their caste or creed, who will one day weld the contending factions into a composite whole, and make of India a great nation."

The influence that Jim Corbett had on my childhood is immeasurable. An orange, ownerless tomcat lived at the end of Burchett Street in Fremont Park. We named him Tiger. And many a later afternoon I spent stalking him through an expanse of vegetation that small boys in the neighborhood called "the jungle." Armed with my family's black box Kodak camera, I would trail the feral Tiger through "the jungle," which couldn't have encompassed more than half an acre. As a student of his habits, I knew more or less where to find him at specific hours of the afternoon. When his whereabouts were still a mystery after I had investigated the area near the garbage cans, picnic tables, sand box, and swings, I would return to "the jungle" and sit with my eyes shut, waiting, and listen for a mockingbird or blue jay to betray his presence. I learned early to rely on birds to assist me in locating Tiger from the infinite Corbett jungle lore that would one day determine the success or failure of more than one of my photographic animal studies.

Such was my imagination that "the jungle" of Fremont Park was interchangeable with the forests of Kumaon, and more than once, after being unsuccessful in locating Tiger, I would turn around to find that he had stalked and was staring through the foliage at me. It was then that I realized just how similar domestic and wild felines are. This recognition made domestic cats even more fascinating to me. Though I used mockingbirds and blue jays to help me track cats like Tiger through Fremont Park, these experiences seemed to only carbon-copy those related in the faded yellow pages of Corbett's books. As I would gaze at Tiger staring at me, I would recall Jim Corbett's words:

"We are likely to forget that the hearing and sight of wild animals, especially of those that depend exclusively on these senses not only for food but also for self-preservation, are on a plane far above that of civilized human beings, and that there is no justification for us to assume that because we cannot hear or see the movements of our prospective quarry, our quarry cannot hear or see our movements. A wrong estimation of the intelligence of animals and the inability to sit without making any sound or movement for the required length of time are the causes of all failures when sitting up for animals. As an example of the acute sense of hearing of carnivora and the care it is necessary to exercise when contact with one of them is desired, I shall relate one of my recent experiences.

"On a day in March when the carpet of dry leaves on the ground recorded the falling of every dead leaf and the movements of the smallest of the birds that feed on the ground, I located—in some very heavy undergrowth—the exact position of a tiger I had long wished to photograph, by moving a troop of langurs in the direction in which I suspected the tiger to be lying up. Seventy yards from the tiger there was an open glade, fifty yards long and thirty yards wide. On the edge of the glade, away from the tiger, there was a big tree overgrown with creepers that extended right up to the topmost branches; twenty feet from the ground the tree forked in two. I knew that the tiger would cross the glade in the late afternoon, for the glade lay directly between him and his sambar kill, which I had found early that morning. As there was no suitable cover near the kill for the tiger to lie up in during the day, he had gone to the heavy undergrowth where the langurs had located him for me.

"It is often necessary, when shooting or photographing tigers and leopards on foot, to know the exact position of the quarry, whether it be a wounded animal that one desires to put out of its misery, or an animal that one wants to photograph, and the best way of doing this is by enlisting the help of birds or animals. With patience, and with a knowledge of their habits, it is not difficult to get a particular bird or animal to go in the required direction. The birds most suitable for this purpose are red jungle fowl, peafowl, and white-capped babblers, and of animals the most suitable are kakar and langurs.

"The tiger I am telling you about was unwounded, and it would have been quite easy for me to go into the undergrowth and find him myself; but in doing so I would have disturbed him and defeated my own purpose, whereas by using the troop of langurs and knowing what their reactions would be on sighting the tiger—if he happened to be in the undergrowth—I was able to get the information I wanted without disturbing the tiger.

"Very carefully I stalked the tree I have referred to, and avoiding contact with the creepers—the upper tendrils and leaves of which might have been visible from where the tiger was lying—I climbed to the fork where I had a comfortable seat and perfect concealment. Getting out my 16 mm. cine camera I made an opening in the screen of leaves in front of me just big enough to photograph through. Having accomplished all this without having made any sound, I sat still; my field of vision was confined to the glade and to the jungle immediately beyond it.

"After I had been sitting for an hour, a pair of bronze-wing doves rose out of the jungle and went skimming over the low brushwood, and a minute or two later, and a little closer to me, a small flight of upland pipits rose off the ground and, after daintily tripping along the branches of a leafless tree, rose above the tree tops and went off. Neither of these two species of birds has any alarm call, but I knew from their behaviour that the tiger was afoot, and that they had been disturbed by him. Minutes later I was slowly turning my eyes from left to right, scanning every foot of ground visible to me, when my eyes came to rest on a small white object, possibly an inch or two square, immediately in front of me, and about ten feet from the edge of the glade. Focusing my eyes on this stationary object for a little while, I then continued to scan the bushes to the limit of my field of vision to the right, and then back again to the white object. 147

"I was now convinced that this object had not been where it was for more than a minute or two before I had first caught sight of it, and that it could not be anything else than a white mark on the tiger's face. Quite evidently the tiger had heard me when I was approaching or climbing the tree, although I had done this in thin rubber shoes without making any sound as far as I was aware; when the time had come for him to go to his kill he had stalked, for a distance of seventy yards over dry leaves, the spot he had pin-pointed as the source of some suspicious sound. After lying for half an hour without making any movement, he stood up, stretched himself, yawned, and then, satisfied that he had nothing to fear, walked out into the glade. Here he stood turning his head first to the right and then to the left, and then, crossing the glade, he passed right under my tree on his way to his kill."

My observations of Tiger and other feral cats was not limited to Fremont Park. During summer vacations with my Uncle Jim and Aunt Fann in San Francisco, early evenings were frequently spent with my uncle's binoculars pressed to my face, zooming me across Masonic Avenue to the abandoned Anza Vista cemetery. Stealthily prowling through the tall weeds and among the tombstones were feral felines, and I followed moment by moment, until the final pounce, as they skillfully stalked California quail, or until my glamorous aunt would call us to the table and Swedish meatballs, the aroma of which had already caused my mouth to water. As we sat down to eat, my uncle would unfailingly ask, "Would you rather smell them or eat them?" after which I would turn the conversation to the cats in the cemetery, hoping the topic would prompt my uncle to tell us of a boyhood experience with mountain lions in Wyoming.

Ernest Hemingway was my idol then, but in college I would never have fantasized that little time would pass before I would be "captured" or taken "prisoner," as he called it, by the white-bearded god of American literature and manhood. That good fortune fell on me during the summer of 1959, and I especially remember an evening that he, American matador-painter John Fulton, and I spent, drinking wine and eating shellfish on a rickety wooden table whose legs were unevenly stuck into sand dampened by the Málaga bay. I felt part of some wonderful dream as, contrary to the objectionable super-macho things I had heard about him, Ernest Hemingway's sensitivity and compassion reached even beyond my expectations. Part of that conversation, lasting until well after midnight, was dedicated to cats, big and small, which I knew Hemingway loved. As he spoke, passages from his stories that I practically knew by memory echoed in my mind:

"Macomber saw the lion now. He was standing almost broadside, his great head up and turned toward them. The early morning breeze that blew toward them was just stirring his dark mane, and the lion looked huge, silhouetted on the rise of bank in the gray morning light, his shoulders heavy, his barrel of a body bulking smoothly. . . .

"Macomber stepped out of the curved opening at the side of the front seat, onto the step and down onto the ground. The lion still stood looking majestically and coolly toward this object that his eyes only showed in silhouette, bulking like some superrhino. There was no man smell carried toward him and he watched the object, moving his great head a little from side to side. Then watching the object, not afraid, but hesitating before going down the bank to drink with such a thing opposite him, he saw a man figure detach itself from it and he turned his heavy head and swung toward the cover of the trees . . ."

At his home in Cuba, Ernest Hemingway kept a large assortment of domestic felines, and he told me how he joyed in watching them hunt and play, feeling as I that the fireside tabby is merely a shrunken lion without a mane.

When I saw Hemingway the following summer in Spain, it was obvious that physically and psychologically he was close to the end of the passionate ride life had given him. Even the year before, I could see how his immense struggle had strained his marriage with his patient wife, Mary. One night, as I left them in the bar of the Miramar Hotel and returned to listen to the waves slapping the glistening moonlit rocks below the window of the pension room, my thoughts centered on Ernest and Mary and on his story "Cat in the Rain":

"The American wife stood at the window looking out. Outside right under their window a cat was crouched under one of the dripping green tables. The cat was trying to make herself so compact that she would not be dripped on.

"'I'm going down and get that kitty,' the American wife said.

"'I'll do it,' her husband offered from the bed.

"'No, I'll get it. The poor kitty out trying to keep dry under a table.'

"The husband went on reading, lying propped up with the two pillows at the foot of the bed.

"'Don't get wet,' he said.

"The wife went downstairs . . .

"The cat would be around to the right. Perhaps she could go along under the eaves. As she stood in the doorway an umbrella opened behind her. It was the maid who looked after their room.

"'You must not get wet,' she smiled, speaking Italian. Of course, the hotel-keeper had sent her.

"With the maid holding the umbrella over her, she walked along the gravel path until she was under their window. The table was there, washed bright green in the rain, but the cat was gone. She was suddenly disappointed. The maid looked up at her.

"'Ha perduto qualche cosa, Signora?'

"'There was a cat,' said the American girl.

"'A cat?'

"'Sì, il gatto.'

"'A cat?' the maid laughed. 'A cat in the rain?'

"'Yes,' she said, 'under the table.' Then, 'Oh, I wanted it so much. I wanted a kitty.'

"When she talked English the maid's face tightened.

"'Come, Signora,' she said. 'We must get back inside. You will be wet.'

"'I suppose so,' said the American girl.

She went on up the stairs. She opened the door of the room. George was on the bed, reading.

"'Did you get the cat?' he asked, putting the book down.

"'It was gone.'

"'Wonder where it went to,' he said, resting his eyes from reading.

"She sat down on the bed.

"'I wanted it so much,' she said. 'I don't know why I wanted it so much. I wanted that poor kitty. It isn't any fun to be a poor kitty out in the rain.'

Not long after that lovely summer in Málaga, luck again brought to my acquaintance a person who would play an important part in my life—Fleur Cowles. First, Fleur not only introduced me to Sir William Collins but also helped convince him to buy my first two books of color photographs. Those were wonderful days in publishing, when houses were owned by people and not by conglomerates; I will never forget flying to London to have lunch with Billy and Pierre Collins. His eyes sparkled as he told me of a recent trip to Africa and camping out with Elsa, the lioness, and with Joy Adamson, whose first book, *Born Free,* he had recently published. Here was a woman who was living my fantasy in Africa with an adult lioness. After the Adamsons had taught Elsa to make her own kills and successfully returned her to the wild came this touching ending to *Born Free.*

"I arrived in Kenya on July 5th. Before the aircraft landed at Nairobi Airport and long before I saw George, I saw our Land Rover; it was by far the most battered car among the shiny limousines in the parking place. However much I may have blushed at other times to be connected with such a shabby vehicle, I felt now deeply moved to see it standing there with all its scratches and dents where Elsa had left her marks. I suggested to George that we should start straight away to visit her, but he convinced me that we ought first to buy a new Land Rover, as our old friend was literally falling to pieces. And so we had to part with this good but decrepit companion which was so much part of Elsa, and bought the latest luxury model, which was of course much more comfortable and respectable. But we wondered how Elsa would react to it.

"George had arranged his local leave to coincide with my return, and soon we were on our way to Elsa. When we arrived at her camp on July 12th, it was already getting dark. About twenty minutes later, while we were putting up my tent, we heard the well-known barking of baboons coming from the river; these always heralded Elsa's arrival.

"George suggested that I should get into the truck until Elsa had used up a little of her energy in greeting him, as he was afraid that in her excitement at seeing me after such a long parting she might not be able to control her great strength and might do me some injury.

"Rather reluctantly I followed his advice and watched her welcome him, but after a few minutes I got out. Suddenly she saw me and, as though it were the most natural thing in the world, walked quietly over from George and started rubbing her

face against my knees and miaowing in her usual way. Then, with claws well tucked in, she used her three hundred pounds to bowl me over, after which she played in her usual friendly way without any fuss or excitement. She has filled out and grown enormously, and I was glad to see that her stomach was full; owing to this it was a long time before she showed any interest in the Grant's gazelle which George had brought. To our surprise, later, she jumped onto the roof of the new, shiny Land Rover with the same matter-of-factness with which she had greeted me, though it looked so very different from the old battered vehicle she was used to.

"For the night we decided that I would put my camp bed into the truck, in case Elsa might feel inclined to share it with me. This proved a wise precaution, for soon after the lamps were turned out she crept determinedly through the thorn fence which surrounded my *boma* and, standing on her hind legs, looked into the truck and satisfied herself that I was there. However, after this she settled down next to the car till early morning; then I heard her dragging the Grant's gazelle carcass down to the riverbank, where she guarded it until George got up and called for breakfast. Then she reappeared and was about to make a flying leap toward me; but when I called, 'No, Elsa, no,' she controlled herself and walked up quietly and, while we ate, sat with one paw touching me. Then she returned to her neglected kill.

"For the next six days Elsa shared our camp routine and our morning and evening walks. One day we watched her stalk a waterbuck while he was drinking on the other side of the river. She froze rigid in a most uncomfortable attitude till he gave her a chance to move swiftly downwind, then, crossing the river without the slightest splash, disappeared in the bush. When she returned she rubbed her head against us as if to tell us about the obvious failure of her hunt. On another occasion we surprised a large bird of prey on the body of a freshly killed dik-dik; when it left its victim we offered this little antelope to Elsa but she refused it, wrinkling up her nose in her usual grimace at anything she does not like. Another time we picnicked downriver for a day's fishing and I sat making sketches of her. As soon as I started eating my sandwiches she insisted on getting her share and tried with her big paws to snatch them from my mouth.

"At other moments she was not so gentle, and we had to be on the alert to avoid her playful ambushes, for she has become so strong now that the impact of her heavy body is certainly no mutual pleasure.

"One morning she had a wonderful game in the river with a stick which George had thrown to her. She retrieved it, leapt in caprioles around it, splashing all the water she could whip up with her tail, dropped the stick again only to have an excuse to dive for it and bring it proudly to the surface. While George was filming her near the water's edge, she pretended not to notice him but cunningly maneuvered herself closer and closer; then she suddenly dropped the stick and leapt on the poor fellow as if to say: 'That's for you, you photographer.' When George tried to get revenge, she hopped away and with unbelievable swiftness climbed a sloping tree trunk out of everyone's reach. There she sat, licking her paws, looking utterly innocent.

"After this performance Elsa paid us only short visits for the next two days and became very detached. On the 23rd she did not come for our morning walk, but in the late afternoon we observed her outlined on the rock ridge near camp and could hardly believe our eyes when we saw a whole troop of baboons within twenty yards, apparently quite unconcerned. Very reluctantly she answered our call and joined us at the foot of the rock, but soon afterward walked away as fast as she could into the bush. We followed until it was dark. Later she came back to us and put up with my patting her but was obviously restless and uneasy and wanted to go off. All that night and the next day she was away, coming only once for a quick meal. The following day while we were talking after supper she suddenly appeared dripping wet from having crossed the river. She greeted George and me affectionately, but while eating her dinner she constantly stopped to listen to something outside. By morning she was gone. This strange behavior puzzled us. She showed no sign of being in season, and we began to wonder whether we had outstayed our welcome. This was far the longest we had spent with her since her release.

"Next evening again at dinnertime Elsa suddenly appeared out of the darkness and with one swish of her tail swept everything off the table; after embracing us with rather excessive affection

she went off into the night, though she returned for a brief moment as if to apologize.

"Next morning the explanation for her strange behavior was written plain in the pugmarks of a large lion. In the afternoon we saw, through our field glasses, a lot of vultures circling and went to investigate; we found the spoors of many hyenas and jackals and the pugmarks of a lion. These led toward the river, where the lion had no doubt drunk and had left a large pool of blood-soaked sand. But there was no sign of Elsa's tracks and no kill to account either for the vultures or for the blood. We spent six hours searching the surrounding area but had to return to camp without solving the mystery. That evening Elsa came in very hungry and spent the night with us, but was gone by dawn.

"On the 29th we saw her on the high rock ridge, and after a few minutes' calling she joined us, purring repeatedly and affectionately, but soon returned to her rock. Now we saw that she was in season, which explained her recent behavior. When we visited her again in the afternoon, although she replied to our calls, she would not come down and we had to climb up the rock. When it was getting dark she got up and as if saying good-bye to us rubbed her head against me, George, and the gun bearer and then walked slowly toward her lie-up. Only once did she look back at us. Next day I saw her through my field glasses resting on her rock. If she could have spoken she could hardly have told us more convincingly that she wanted to be left alone. However much affection we gave her, it was plain she

needed the company of her own kind.

"We decided to break camp. As our two cars passed below her rock, she appeared on the skyline and watched us driving away.

"Our next visit to Elsa was between the 18th and 23rd of August. She was as usual most affectionate while she was with us, but out of these five days she spent two alone in the bush and, although we did not see the spoor of a lion, she seemed to prefer solitude to sharing our life. It was of course best for her that she should become independent of our ties.

"On the 29th of August George was obliged to go to Elsa's area for Game control and arrived at 6 P.M. at her camp to spend the night there. He fired off two thunder flashes to attract her attention. At about 8 P.M. he heard a lion downriver and let off another thunder flash. The lion continued to call throughout the night, but there was no sign of Elsa. Next morning George found the pugmarks of a young lion or lioness close to camp. He had to leave immediately afterward but returned at 4 P.M. An hour later Elsa came across the river, looking very fit and full of affection. Although she was not hungry, she ate a little of the buck which George had brought her and then dragged the carcass into the tent. Soon after dark a lion began to call. Much to George's surprise, she completely ignored the invitation, which continued throughout most of the night.

"Early next morning she made a hearty meal and then without any show of hurry disappeared in the direction from which the lion had called.

Shortly afterward George heard her voice and saw her sitting on a big rock and heard her making deep grunts. As soon as she spotted him, she came down and met him but, although pleased to see him, made it obvious that she wanted to be alone and after a brief head-rubbing disappeared into the bush. Guessing the direction she had taken, George followed and found her running tracks heading for the river. Presently he saw her sitting on a rock almost hidden by bush. He watched her for some time. She seemed very restless and kept on looking intently downstream. First she miaowed, then with a startled "whuff-whuff" dashed down the rock and streaked past George into the bush. Next moment a young lion appeared, evidently in hot pursuit, and not sensing George came straight toward him. When the lion was less than twenty yards away George thought it time to act and waved his arms and shouted. Startled, the beast spun around and made off the way he had come. A few seconds later Elsa reappeared, squatted nervously close to George for a few moments, and then followed the lion. George withdrew and moved camp.

"Two days later he had to revisit the same area. A few hundred yards before reaching Elsa's camp one of the men in the car saw her under a bush close to the track, apparently hiding: most unusual behavior, for normally she would rush out to meet the car and greet everyone. Thinking the man might have mistaken a wild lioness for Elsa, George turned the car and drove back. There she was sitting under the bush. At first she made no

movement; then, realizing that she had been caught out, she came forward and was courtesy itself, making a great fuss of George and pretending to be as pleased as ever at seeing him, and she condescended to eat some of the meat he had brought her. While she was eating, George walked up the track to look for spoor. He found her pugmarks together with those of another lion. Then he saw the lion himself peeping at him from behind a bush. It appeared to be the same one which he had seen with Elsa a few days earlier. Presently there was an uproar from a troop of baboons by the river, which heralded the approach of the lion. Hearing this, Elsa hurriedly finished her meal and went off to find her lord and master.

"George went on and pitched camp and left the remainder of the meat in the tent for Elsa, before going on to do his work. On his return to camp the meat was still untouched and Elsa did not appear during the night.

"At last Elsa has found her mate, and perhaps our hopes will be fulfilled and one day she may walk into camp followed by a litter of strapping cubs."

Billy Collins added this postscript:

"Publisher's Note:

"As the culmination of this story, at the end of December we received the following cable: CUBS BORN 20TH—ADAMSON."

When I visited Fleur Cowles and her husband, Tom, in London, I was completely taken by her paintings, most of which were inhabited by big cats. Not only did they vibrate with color but they had a rare imaginative quality that I had never before encountered in graphic renditions of animals. It was then that I proposed we do a book together, but Fleur said she was a painter and not an illustrator, and so would not feel comfortable trying to express ideas on canvas other than her own.

Visualizing the book and unwilling to leave London without some chance at doing it, I convinced Fleur to obtain Ektachromes of as many of her paintings as possible, most of which were scattered in collections throughout the world. Months later, as my light table rainbowed with color, I put unrelated paintings into order, after which I wrote a tale around them to create *Tiger Flower*, which was followed by *Lion and Blue*.

The fact that both *Tiger Flower* and *Lion and Blue* were elected by the American Booksellers Association and the American Association of Librarians to a list of the ten children's books of all time with most adult appeal, a list that includes *The Little Prince*, would certainly swell the pride of any author. However, the praise that most delighted my ears came from Paul Gallico, when he wrote that he found *Tiger Flower* "absolutely enchanting," adding, "I look at it again and again." Paul Gallico I had long admired. If Jim Corbett captures the spirit of the tiger, Gallico is certainly his equal when it comes to describing the domestic cat. No one has ever so perceptively deciphered the beauty of the cat:

"If it is true that beauty lieth in the eye of the beholder then the continuous and manifold appeal of the cat lieth most felicitously in mine and the word comes into its fullest interpretation. Everything a cat is and does physically is to me beautiful, lovely, stimulating, soothing, attractive, and an enchantment.

"It begins, I should say, with the compactness of construction, composition, size, proportion, and general overall form. The domesticated cat is the tidiest of all animals. There is an almost divine neatness and economy about the animal. Completely packaged in fur with not a bald spot showing, rarely two specimens wholly alike, it often comes decorated with designs that Picasso might envy and always functionally streamlined for every activity; just another case of the practical made glamorous.

"I will not deny you that there are beautiful dog faces, some with expressions that pierce you directly to the heart, but the dog has been bred into some weirdo sizes and shapes of body, some of which must cause the poor animal considerable embarrassment. With the cat the arrangement of eyes, nose, mouth, and ears is superbly drawn to give the utmost satisfaction to the beholder, and the eyes themselves with their depth and mystery are deserving of a chapter alone. Nobody has ever managed to breed the cat into an ugly shape with the possible exception of that genetic sport the Manx cat, tailless and with its hind legs slightly out of plumb, reminiscent of the bunny rabbit. One feels sorry for this accident. To fulfill its definition a cat wants a tail, so that one's eye can travel easily along its lithe body from the tip of its whiskers to the gracefully waving appendage.

"It is not true to say that there are no ugly cats; there are indeed occasionally squint-eyed, ill-favored creatures decorated with badly mismatched colors and even sometimes misshapen. But if you can put up with the paradox, to me, as the animal still remains a cat, it still retains its measure of beauty. Furthermore it doesn't know it is ugly and thus my heart goes out to it. Also, its mother loves it.

"Except for the bright-plumaged birds, the cat surpasses all specimens of the animal kingdom including, I must add, ourselves, in the variety of hues and design.

"It all began as protective coloration and jungle camouflage, and your tabby still persists in the stripes that were developed to make it invisible against thickets and bamboos and reeds. The wall paintings of the Egyptian cats show this pattern to predominate.

"But down through some four thousand years from B.C. to A.D. the cat by natural selection must have been preparing itself for modern times and modern eyes in shades and patterns. To the pure white and the almost totally black (you know, of course, that there is no such thing as a wholly black cat; you always find at least a few white hairs on his chest to keep it out of the hands of the witches) are now added the ginger, the red tabby, the *café-au-lait* Siamese with its eyes of exquisite translucent blue shining from a black mask, the grays, the silvers, the browns and blues, and the surrealistic mixtures of the calico cat as well as other crazy-quilt numbers resulting from some of the more casual adventures in love.

"Plato characterized beauty by measure and

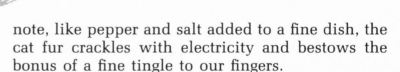

symmetry, Plotinus as being the supremacy of the higher over the lower, of form and matter, and Cicero, as distinguished from the useful and compromising as distinct types of dignity and charm and grace. Old Noah Webster dissects the word *beauty* as an assemblage of graces or properties or some one of them satisfactory to the eye, the intellect, the aesthetic faculty, and the moral sense; also abstract quality characteristic of such properties.

"But Mr. Webster, who may never have owned a cat, leaves out 'touch,' important to any definition and which, however, is included among the sensuous qualities. Oh, yes, there is no question but what the fur of the cat is pleasing to touch and, circa the turn of the century, therapeutic to bronchial troubles when worn next to the skin on the chest, separated, however, from the cat before applying. It is more than pleasing, namely alluring, seductive, and irresistible, the latter in the sense that if you are not a phobe, it is almost impossible *not* to stroke a cat that comes within range.

"Humans, like the monkey, are all touchers; we need to receive messages tactilely through the ends of our fingers, and one of the most pleasurable of such communications is between cat and oneself as one passes one's hand over its sleek body. I believe the psychiatrists lift an eyebrow at this and mutter something about sexual connotations which I am not prepared to argue since sex can be beautiful too. Soft is good. And when the cat pushes its firm but delicate little skull wrapped in softness, as it were, against the heel of our hand, the effect is delightful; and sometimes, as a grace

note, like pepper and salt added to a fine dish, the cat fur crackles with electricity and bestows the bonus of a fine tingle to our fingers.

"I consider few sounds more gratifying than a purr, unless it be that divine melody sung by a happy feline which combines both purr and a little cry, the well-known 'Prrrrrrrr-mow!'

"The purr is an indescribable sound, and this forced combination of letters, namely 'prrrrrr,' does it no justice. One can only refer to the sense of joy and tranquility experienced by the purrer and transferred to the soul of the listener. There are times, though regrettably not too many, when we ourselves would purr if we could. Yet, with all our faculties, we simply have no way of expressing our completest satisfaction with the moment to compare with that of House Cat.

"The purr is beautiful! I doubt whether it could be properly reproduced, say, even by the most delicate electronic recorder. It would come out as some other kind of noise since the machine's mechanical heart simply would be unable to reproduce all the internal vibrations provided by the contentment of the cat, and our human ear would very quickly detect the counterfeit.

"I will admit that there is nothing harmonious or attractive about a catfight. But the back fence nighttime melody of wooing has its moment, provided you are not an irritable person dead bent on getting to sleep. The appeal lies in its primitiveness and naturalness. Surely all men at some time when they have been in love have wished that they might sing to the object thereof, to pour forth under her window the fullness and the glory

of the emotion she has aroused in them. One is aware that if one did one would be cutting a ridiculous figure, nor would the noises emerging from one's throat do the trick.

"Not so the cat. When so moved, he simply sings and his lady loves it. When the earth was very young and the antediluvian carnivores were a-prowl, the endless savannas of the wilderness must have echoed to such music. Something in our ears and hearts can remember it.

"Again with the aesthetic faculty appealed to, beauty offers the combination of the sublime, the tragic, and the comic. The cat offers me all three, present either singly or in combination. Sublime is an empyrean word, but there are moments when the cat is entitled to it, for there are few expressions that can match those on the face of Mother House Cat as she tends her young, or presents them, or even prepares for delivery. And as for the tragic, you will have to seek far for a greater sadness, gallantry, and nobility than that of a long-time friend, an old cat at its dying. A starving, ill-treated specimen has the power to arouse our sympathies almost to the extent of that of a cruelly treated child. For all the pampering that accrues to the lucky one, cats in a sense are waifs in the world, each and every one a candidate for adoption. Those that fail to achieve it are the tragic figures.

"And withal, and still within the definition of beauty, the comic is never far from the surface of the animal. Cats are funny. They have always appealed to humorists, cartoonists, and poets.

"A cat's comedy is unconscious, slightly rueful, and often delicate. You have only to make the egregious error of laughing out loud, instead of enjoying the moment inwardly, to destroy it. You will also insult your cat almost beyond redemption and it will be days before you are forgiven; it cannot bear to be laughed *at*. But you must not mind if its sense of humor manifests itself in taking advantage of your own weaknesses, foibles, or inabiity to measure up.

"Cats don't laugh; they do grin as anyone familiar with Lewis Carroll and *Alice* knows, but even the grin of the Cheshire Cat, and for that matter any cat, is suspect since it may be an expression connected with something quite different, such as the various emotions ascribed to a baby because of that look that comes over its face just before it is about to be untidy.

"But the cat definitely has its funny moments, even almost up to the point of near-hysteria, when it suddenly seems to go mad and flies all over the premises, up and down curtains, in and around and over furniture at high speeds, only to stop suddenly, look around at you with an expression that may be accurately determined as 'Hasn't this been a lark?' The cat that decides not to come in at night and leads you on a nocturnal chase you know is laughing its head off at you every time you grab and miss, and the madder you get, the more successful the joke.

"But as I have said, you must not return the compliment. If your cat gets itself entangled in something, or falls over while washing or can't get its Ping-Pong ball from under the couch, do, for the sake of a harmonious household, keep a straight face. I have encountered clown cats who 157

wanted to be the center of attraction and who didn't mind that you shouted with laughter at their antics, but this type most definitely lets us know. It is the unconscious and basic gaiety of the cat that verges on beauty.

"And so finally to the last word connected with the formal beauty of these animals, namely their attitudes. Attitudes and poses! The former are natural, the latter deliberate. There are, for instance, all the various positions for washing, too well known to be redescribed, but there are several in particular which come to my mind such as when the cat swivels its head almost ninety degrees on its neck and then with long sweeping strokes works its long tongue down over its shoulders and spine. And what movement is more charming than that in which the side of the paw is moistened and then rubbed vigorously over an ear?

"An attitude need not be static. A cat running is a flow of rhythm and coordination which, in a moment, can be turned to the most amusing burlesque when it decides to gallop and bring its padded feet down hard upon the floor. Or is there any lazier or more luxurious movement than a cat getting up and stretching? Always, always, is the eye diverted and the intellect of appreciation stimulated by movement. House Cat jumping, pouncing, playing, rolling, cruising; each of these has its moments of supreme delectation. Nothing the animal does is ungraceful.

"But I think a cat at rest with me in the same room is what I like best. The curl-up in a perfect circle or sometimes with one paw over its eyes as though to shut out the light; the hunker with all

four feet tidily tucked under, or the sit-up with its tail neatly tucked around its bottom. The poses I know are sheer vanity, for cats are indeed vain and like to be admired. But they will choose backgrounds and put themselves into positions which they know are admirable. They will drape their bodies to the shape of a piece of furniture. They will hang a paw in what seems to be a wholly casual manner, but you know and they know damn well that it is studied. But it is never wrong. Merely by the turn of their heads upon their necks, a half an inch or so, they can change the picture and give expression to some inner feeling and, by doing so, set up a glow of appreciation in the watcher.

"Well, and as for words, they define less than House Cat illustrates them: aesthetic, sublime, tragic, comic, symmetry, supremacy, dignity, charm and grace; in short, the beautiful."

On the controversial subject of cruelty and cats, Paul Gallico is equally sage:

"Of course, the grand joke in discussing the much referred to 'cruelty' of house or barn cat at work is the inclusion of the word 'inhuman' in its list of synonyms, namely, 'harshness, brutality, ruthlessness, barbarity, inhumanity, atrocity.'

"The case immediately collapses and kitty is entitled to laugh its head off every time it hears the word applied to itself, what it does, and how. For cruelty is one of the specialties of the human, since it is with deliberation, forethought, and the knowledge that we are indifferent to or, in the definition of the word, disposed to take pleasure in the pain or distress of another, or to show ourselves hardhearted and pitiless. We know better and yet have remained specialists in the practice thereof.

"The charges brought against the cat are based purely upon observation of its hunting tactics. This and the fact that it includes birds among its prey: the reputation of the cat has suffered mostly from the highly vocal lobby of the bird lovers. And once again it is necessary to point out that bird lovers are people. Worms, fish, insects, frogs, snakes, and small rodents that are attacked by birds, carried off, mangled horribly, and then eaten are not exactly included among the worshippers of our feathered friends.

"It all boils down rather to who eats whom. Since the bird lover will sit down to a tasty dish of partridge, quail or pheasant while his heart bleeds for the sparrow, the robin, or the linnet which is less edible, the situation is likely to become confused. One thing, however, is certain; if you separate the word *cruelty* from deliberate intent and consider only results, the bird is as cruel as the cat and, furthermore, is one up in that it can attack via another dimension.

"'Like a cat playing with a mouse!' You know that phrase. Falsely worded. It should be—like a cat 'practicing' or 'training' with a mouse.

"Gentlemen hunters used to practice their skill with wing shots using live pigeons released from a trap until the advent of the clay disk that serves the same purpose. Before we became aware that we were destroying all wild animal life in our presence, game was shot for the fun of it and to increase one's efficiency, rather than for the pot.

"The cat is a hunter for food and the instinct has never been bred out of it. Games with an injured prey have nothing to do with the will to cause it pain and suffering. There are two main objectives; to keep the hunting muscles and speed and timing sharp, or to bring a no longer dangerous specimen to its kittens for similar exercises. As to the latter tactic, one remembers that the picadors injure the bull before he is turned over to the mercies of the brave matador.

"Almost all of a cat's 'play' is not play at all, but practice. Its immediate interest in anything small that moves, a leaf, a blade of grass stirred by the wind, a flutter of paper, a thistledown, is reflex. If it moves it may be alive, if alive and small it may be catchable and edible.

"There are the hunter and the hunted and let the hunted beware in the inexorable hierarchy of Nature. The cat stalking the field mouse in the meadow should not forget the eagle or the goshawk hovering in the sky.

"But let us confine ourselves to the mouse which has its own endowments of speed, scent, cunning, and instinct and is often smart enough to move himself and his family out of the house when cat moves in. Try getting down on your elbows and knees to catch a mouse with your bare hands. You won't, but if you should succeed, you are likely to get bitten and, if it should be a rat, you might die of the bite. Well, we are smarter and know our limitations. We invent and set a trap for the mouse, treacherously baited with its favorite dish. The spring trap if it does not hit just the right angle lets the mouse linger at its dying all through the night.

"The cat has to work it all on its own, with skill, concealment, judgment of distance, and speed. It must strike like lightning. Have you watched your cat, as you trail a piece of paper tied to string across the floor, waggle its bottom before it pounces? The boxer, the fencer, the football, baseball, and tennis player have all learned that one moves more quickly out of movement than from the stationary.

"Infinite patience, perfect timing are involved in a successful mouse hunt; savvy, planning, plus absolute muscular control.

"But at no time is the cat emotionally involved with the mouse. It has neither knowledge of nor interest in how the mouse feels about it. Nor are there that many mice about, nor does the cat always win. There are fast and savvy mice too. Thus, one caught and not wholly disabled by the first pounce becomes a valuable prize and training adjunct. But sheer thoughtless, heedless, or planned and intended cruelty as we know of it today, by our own standards, is no part of the picture. Even a tree may suffer agonies when it is cut down. We have no way of knowing, and if we did, we would still cut down trees.

"A bird, is a bird, is a bird, as it might have appeared to the late Miss Stein, but to a cat it is a meal and not only a meal but the superchallenge. The fact that it sings beautifully doesn't interfere with its flavor, or that soaring in the heavens or perched on a leafy branch it is a delight to the eye.

The cat would never understand the practice of keeping such a dinner caged during its lifetime.

"It might even consider this to come under the head of that mysterious word used so lightly by humans—'cruelty.'"

In conclusion, Paul Gallico's words on love and the cat are certainly the most poignant ever written:

"I have one final problem I would like to discuss with you. I sometimes wish I knew what my cat thinks of or feels for me. Or do I? And do you ever, and ought we perhaps to leave well enough alone and not pry?

"I have loved my cats with a curious kind of affection unlike that of any other emotion that I have experienced for man or beast and one which I have never, up to this point, tried to analyze, dissect, or understand. And now that I try to do so I think that it is compounded of admiration, sympathy, and amusement. To this I add a slight and curious tincture of pity plus a wholly unpredictable and irrational feeling which comes welling up out of depths indefinable.

"Somewhere, sometime, this extraordinary thing happened between humans and felines.

"Looking backward, our original association was simply mutually and practically rewarding and wholly unsentimental. When first man learned to store his grain he found that mice got into it. The cat was a hunger and small rodents his natural prey. Clever man therefore engaged a cat to help him save his food by putting it where it could hunt to its heart's content and serve man by doing so.

"We know that this situation obtained in Egypt so long ago because this is the first record in painting and writing that we have of this relationship. It is most curious. Primitive man was beginning to save up food long before the Pharaohs. Dog helped him to hunt, but there is no record of cat assisting him to store.

"On the banks of the Nile then, where originally was established this perfect mutual arrangement and balance, one day or one millennium something inexplicable happened; the ferocious guardian of the granaries became a cold, distant, high-placed and worshipped god in the temples.

"The cat in those times was even further involved with humans in that it performed the service eventually usurped by the bird dog and accompanied its owner on the hunt as testified by wall paintings showing a definitely striped tabby lurking in the reeds of the swamps to put up a bird. And not only that but the animal was further willing to act as retriever after the hunter had brought down the quarry with an arrow, spear, or throwing-stick. It didn't take too long to discover it was being conned.

"All in all, for an animal which up to that time appeared not to have been heard of, or noticed, it accomplished the neatest trick of the ages of which the most astonishing and enduring was the manner in which it crept into the hearts and minds of men, women, and children and established itself in the home, and there inspired not only awe, worship, and respect, but above everything else that mattered—love. The paintings and the written records show that the ancient Egyp-

tians pampered and spoiled their house cats, treated them as honored guests, and loved them. But did the cats love the Egyptians, and when and how did that love come about in the breast of that feral creature, or wherever the seat of that emotion might be, and does my cat love me?

"I raise the question, because whereas it is easy for those of us so constituted to be drawn toward those soft, beautiful, and admirable animals, if I were of their species, I think I would find man very difficult to love.

"In fact, taking my cat's point of view, it ought to regard me as something of an unstable and capricious lunatic, stupid, unpredictable, tyrannical, and utterly selfish; satisfactory for board and lodging and an occasional caress, but for the rest utterly useless.

"Well, admitted that uselessness is no bar to affection as many men have discovered, what, besides food and shelter, have I to offer to my four-footed companion except that human type of possessive love that even humans eventually find cloying and my cat certainly does.

"By and large they will take just so much of it. When we love members of our own species we take them in our arms and press them to our hearts. Cats don't like to be squeezed. For that matter they do not care for any manner of confinement and will only rest quiescent in one's grasp for a period they consider polite before starting a scramble for the floor.

"They will take only so much petting, tickling, rubbing, or mauling before, smothering a yawn, they will walk away with a firmness that is unmis-

takable. And if still you fail to get the message, they will either leave the room entirely, or produce a toy from where it has been stashed beneath the bureau and start a game.

"A gentleman cat who loves a lady cat embraces her right enough in what is a combination of a football charge and an all-in wrestling match at the climax of which the object of his amour gets a severe bite in her neck. But we are not considering that kind of love. And besides, when our cat does give it to us, that is to say, when in play we sometimes unwittingly stimulate it sexually and it digs the claws of all four feet into our arm and gives our hand a nip as well, we yell blue murder and accuse the animal of being false, sly, and treacherous.

"It is a human fallacy, the belief that love must engender love and the like, in intensity, to that bestowed. This illusion has been getting men into trouble with women and themselves ever since the emotion was discovered and classified. 'But I love you so,' pleads the unhappy and idiot swain. 'How can you possibly not love me in return?' And even when there exists a mutuality of affection, people lovers want to make it quantitative. 'Do you love me as much as I love you?' They wish to put it onto a scale and see whether it balances or which way it tips. We at least can find out linguistically or lie decently to one another. But my wise, dumb animal isn't saying.

"And so I wonder whether it has the mechanism of love, the kind of which I am thinking; unphysical, abstract, yet deeply felt, surging and impelling, the kind which is not 'made' but which simply happens when the object thereof comes within range.

"For there is always the lurking sensation in all of us of the power of the cupboard. Was there in bygone days a real cat deity, a supercat who one moment, smitten with a stroke of genius, discovered and imparted to all that followed it that man is the eternal sucker who can be flattered or conned into anything with the right approach? When ofttimes we are compelled to the same doubts as to the sincerity of the fervent declarations of undying passion from members of our own kind, what is so strange in suspecting that our cat maybe is putting on the act of the ages? In fact, one would have to be wholly besotted with one's own worth *not* to wonder, knowing the cat's reserve and independence. Suspicion is further an outgrowth of the fact that they can turn it on and they can turn it off. And if for the most part you seem to remember that they turn it on when there would appear to be something in it for them, then you suddenly remember that day when you sat depressed in a chair, suffering from a hurt concealed, a worry, a disappointment, or a crisis, and suddenly there was someone soft and furry in your lap and a body pressed close to yours in warmth and comfort.

"Or there is the presentation mouse which would come wrapped in white tissue and tied with a golden ribbon if a cat could. Or the waiting by the gate or door for you to come home or some other strange mark of unselfish feeling. Everyone who has ever kept a cat has a story to tell in proof.

"I wrote earlier of the element of pity that was

a part of the emotion I feel and sometimes wonder whether it is not upon this level that mutuality is established and that my wise and well-adjusted cat is feeling sorry for me and would like to help me to be more like its quiet and contented self.

"The true animal lover will understand my use of the word pity, not in the sense of patronizing, for in that there is nothing akin to love, but rather a sympathy with and for them, for their lot, which is not an easy one anymore than is ours. It will be then just as easy to love a hippopotamus as much as a prize Persian, or a jackal, dingo, or hyena as much as a Seal Point Siamese or a silver tabby. More so, perhaps, since the former haven't got it so good and need it so much more.

"No, this compassion, I think, stems from the fact that in one way or another, we are all in the same trap of life cycle and in the short time allotted us are trying to make out the best we can. And the cat more often than not has a hard row to hoe.

"This creature is also the least insistent upon pity which in itself is attractive and breeds the respect that is often the backbone of love. While it is constantly demanding the best, we have seen that it will also do without. The cat can be spoiled rotten, but basically life has taught it to expect little. It is a master of survival on its own terms. It may be an expert at panhandling you or tugging at your heart, but it is always to be remembered that essentially it promises nothing in return, and then suddenly, at the most surprising and unexpected of moments, gives freely.

"Well, there you are, and as the saying goes,

we have come a 'fur piece' from the beginning of the journey without getting any forrader. One starts out by reflecting upon one's house pet and winds up with a self-analysis that is not too flattering with genuine communication reduced to a few signals affording only rare and actually reliable glimpses into the mind and heart of one's cat. And if out of this one is able to salvage something at least slightly admirable in oneself as voluntary associates of this creature, it is the fact that one, in some measure, is able to bear to love something or someone without expecting a return."

During these past fifty years, my life has been enriched not only by cats but by varying forms of contact with some of the world's most famous cat lovers, as well as with regular folk who were equally distinguished because of the affection they poured on their animals. I have enjoyed the company of some beautiful women, from Deborah Kerr to Bo Derek, who were not only feline in their softness and beauty, but in their adoration of the species. I did have contact with another Nobel Prize winner besides Hemingway, Dr. Albert Schweitzer, though only through a letter written to me on his behalf by one of his nurses. In early manhood I wrote to volunteer my services to Lambaréné. My services were not needed, but I was later intrigued to learn that Dr. Schweitzer had learned to write with his right hand to avoid disturbing a cat that might be sleeping on his left arm. So he and I shared a reverence for the cat!

Jim Corbett I deeply regret never having met and, like the Indian soldier's father described in this

163

book, I will have to be satisfied with having shook a hand that once shook his. My great friend Tess LaTouche met Corbett in India when he was instructing troops in jungle lore during World War II.

"Cat music" that has given me pleasure most of my life is the Bagheera theme written by Miklos Rozsa for the Korda version of *Jungle Book,* which starred Sabu. I prevailed on my friend the composer Elmer Bernstein to introduce me to Dr. Rozsa so I might express my gratitude for music that has had a lifelong effect on me and my work. Tea was arranged and, instead of the half hour that had been allotted us, we spent almost two hours with Dr. Rosza as he answered my years-of-waiting questions about the filming of the Korda classic. As we left his mansion high in the Hollywood Hills, which reminded me of the Gloria Swanson house in *Sunset Blvd.,* I was heady with the experience—and this even after we had turned onto Sunset Boulevard, with its foot traffic of punksters representing the new Hollywood.

As work on this book drew to a close, something Peter Ustinov had written in a foreword to one of my previous books was reinforced again and again in every experience I had with cat people who had meaningful relationships with their animals. "Perhaps it is true to say," wrote Ustinov, "that this collection of poetic fragments expresses the most necessary and most underrated of virtues, that of mutual respect. The mutual respect between boy and horse and eventually the respect of the boy for the liberty of the horse, are philosophical attitudes of great beauty and great subtlety,

artistically concealed among the more obvious attractions, the blinding fields of flowers, the jagged silhouettes of rocks and grass, the tremulous pallor of the moon. . . ." Identical would be the words to describe the relationships of most of the people and animals in this book. Beyond the color and exoticness of the images lies respect. This was most obvious with the big cats, as exemplified by Penny and Bill Andrews with their mountain lions and clouded leopards. The cats demand no more of the Andrews than respect and affection, and the Andrews request no more of their cats than the same. There is no training, no situations in which the animals are pushed into stress and respond aggressively. Penny and Bill enter the enclosures without asking the cats to stand on pedestals or jump through fiery hoops—their only interactions are gentle head rubs between man and beast that show friendship and mutual respect.

Last summer on my ranch in Spain, we enjoyed the company for a short while of Chica, a lion cub, and I can still envision her in the evening, curled up on my mother's lap, a small innocent creature whose destiny had denied her freedom but she did at least enjoy the respect and affection of my mother, who represents humanity in its purest and most noble form. This was yet another example of the kind of relationship between feline and human that my boyhood dreams had been built on. My mother may not have allowed Fury in the house, but forty years later she had a lion on her lap and adored it.

In doing this book, I feel I have only begun to

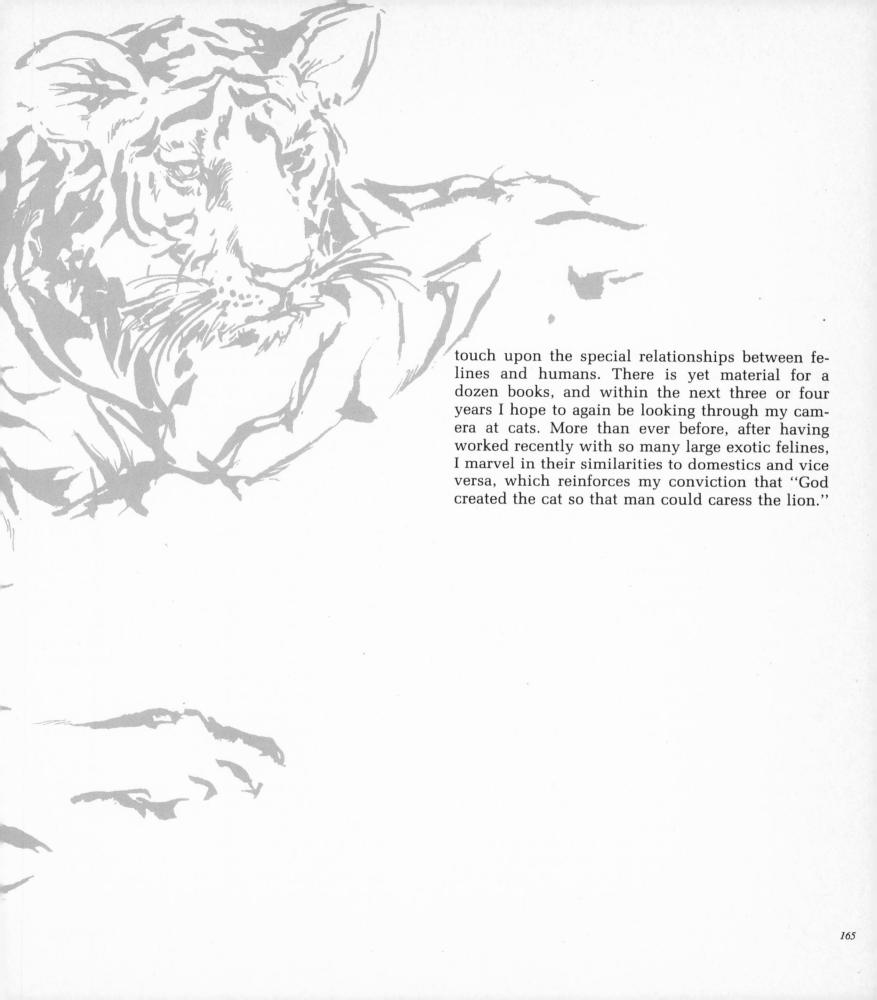

touch upon the special relationships between felines and humans. There is yet material for a dozen books, and within the next three or four years I hope to again be looking through my camera at cats. More than ever before, after having worked recently with so many large exotic felines, I marvel in their similarities to domestics and vice versa, which reinforces my conviction that "God created the cat so that man could caress the lion."

THE PHOTOGRAPHS

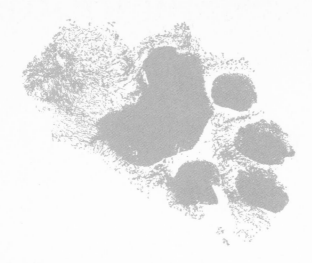

Identification of animals in the photographs is listed here along with certain bits of information on cats. I thank Penny Andrews for the use of the notes she sent me; *PA* identifies such materials as hers. The photographs were taken with two Nikon F3 cameras, using Kodak 400 ASA Ektachrome film.

Page 5
Silver Mau: *Felis Catus*

Comments: This cat's history most likely goes back to ancient Egypt, where it was depicted graphically as early as 1400 B.C. It is also uniquely spotted like no other breed of domestic cat. The modern Egyptian mau dates back to 1953, when Princess Natalie Troubetzkoy imported a female to Italy, where she mated it to another Egyptian and obtained two kittens. It is called Egyptian mau because in ancient Egyptian *mau* means "cat." It is probably a first cousin of the Abyssinian, and comes in three colors: silver, bronze, and smoke.

The Egyptian cat-goddess Bast (also Pasht or Bastet) was represented with the head of a cat. Bast was the daughter of Isis, goddess of the earth and the moon, and Osiris, god of the sun and Isis's brother. The earliest image dates back to around 3000 B.C. Her temple was at the sacred city Bubastis; however, all cats, not only the temple ones, were worshiped and respected in Egypt. Killing cats was punishable by death.

Egyptians believed that a cat's eyes waxed and waned with the moon and the tides; Bast was the goddess of the new moon. Currently in Great Britain maus are bred to have marks on their brows that resemble a scarab, which was another sacred symbol in ancient Egypt.

Page 7
White Tigress: *Panthera Tigris*

Characteristics: weight varies considerably from two hundred fifty to five hundred pounds; head and body length five to six feet; tail two to three feet

Habitat: all types of forest, grassy jungle, marshes, bamboo thickets, rocky areas

Habits: hunts mainly on the ground during both night and day

Prey: antelope, deer, buffalo, monkeys, domestic animals; sometimes birds, frogs, some insects

Distribution: India to Siberia and Southeast Asia

Comments: White tigers are extremely rare in the wild. Jim Corbett reports having observed only one. Some are true albinos, pure white with pink eyes, while others have pale body color and lighter-than-normal markings. The first recorded white tiger to be captured alive and photographed was in 1915 in what was then known as the Rewa State of India. Thereafter others were seen, the most famous of which was a male captured in

1951 by the Maharajah of Rewa, who with it started a breeding program. The white male was bred to a normal-colored tigress, and all of their offspring were orange and black. The white tiger was then bred to one of his daughters and produced his first white cubs. The first offspring were sent to the Bristol Zoo in England and to the National Zoo in Washington, D.C. The legendary illusionists Siegfried and Roy have a superb installation for their white tiger—breeding program in Las Vegas.

Page 9
Sky with clouds

Comments: It is fascinating to imagine the circumstances of that first encounter between man and the small wild feline that would later be known as *Felis Catus domestica.* What is certain, however, is that by the time of their first friendly rendezvous man had advanced to the point of being able to instill trust in the cat—the basic ingredient for the beginning of their association. No one has better described this than Karel Capek: "Among human beings a cat is merely a cat; among cats a cat is a prowling shadow in a jungle. . . . A cat is not simply a cat, but something mysterious and unfathomable; a cat is a wild animal. . . . A cat which does not trust a person, does not see him as a man but a wild animal. The fabric of mutual trust

is older than the whole of civilization, and mankind remains mankind; but if you destroy the state of trust, the world of human beings becomes a land of wild animals. . . . A wild animal is an animal which has no faith. Domestication is simply a state of coincidence."

Pages 10 and 11
Cat and Moon: *Felis Catus*

Characteristics: weight variable depending on the breed, generally seven pounds; head, body, and tail length about one and a half feet, except in the case of bobtail or tailless cats

Habits: hunts during day and night while mostly on the ground, on occasion on low structures and trees

Prey: mice, birds, insects, gophers, rabbits, and other rodents and reptiles

Distribution: worldwide

Comments: It is generally speculated that the domestic cat resulted from a cross between the European wildcat *(Felis sylvestis)* and the African wildcat *(Felis libyca).* It belongs to the mammal class, carnivorous order, Felidae family, *Felis* genus, and *Felis catus* species. *Felis domestica* is the modern cat's scientific name.

Pages 12 and 13
Leopard: *Panthera Pardus*

Characteristics: weight seventy to one hundred twenty pounds; head and body measurement about forty-eight inches; tail about twenty-four inches; spotted or black when melanistic gene is present

Habitat: found in every type of terrain and up to snow line in mountains

Habits: hunts in early morning, late afternoon, and at night

Prey: diversified—large birds, baboons, jackals, small cats, antelope, deer, hares, livestock

Distribution: Africa to Southeast Asia

Longevity: up to twenty years in captivity

Comments: Since man first took to wearing clothing, leopards have been killed for their exotic pelts, and they are not difficult prey for the expert hunter. Corbett says, "Leopards, other than man-eaters, are the most easily killed of all our jungle animals, having a poor sense of smell. The tracking, locating, and stalking of leopards, besides being exciting and interesting, is comparatively easy. Leopards have tender pads and keep to footpaths and game tracks as far as possible. They are not hard to locate; practically every bird and animal in the jungle assists the hunter for though they are blessed with keen sight and hearing, they are handicapped by having no keen sense of smell. The sportsman can therefore select the time of approach that best suits him, irrespectively of the direction in which the wind is blowing.

"Having tracked, located, and stalked a leopard, far more pleasure is got from pressing the button of a camera than is ever got from pressing a trigger of a rifle. In one case the leopard can be watched for hours—and there is no more graceful and interesting animal in the jungle to watch—and the button of a camera can be pressed as fancy dictates and a record secured that never loses its interest. In the other case of a fleeting glimpse, one press of the trigger and—if the aim has been true—the acquisition of a trophy that soon loses its beauty and its interest."

In captivity the leopard is considered the most dangerous, and least predictable, of all big cats.

PA: Generally believed to be the most efficient hunting machine of all the cats. Armand Denis has said, "On the ground they are exceedingly nervous . . . once up a tree the leopard believes himself to be invisible. He relaxes." More dangerous than lions and tigers because of their greater intelligence, agility, and power. "Never trust a spotted cat" is a term that originated with leopards and jaguars.

Page 14
African Lion: *Panthera Leo*

Characteristics: weight three hundred to four hundred pounds; head and body length eight to nine feet; tail two to three feet

Habitat: grassy plains, open woodlands, bush, semidesert

Habits: hunts by day and night; terrestrial and territorial

Prey: mostly hoofed animals and some domestic animals

Distribution: Africa south of the Sahara

Comments: Long fascinated man with its majestic beauty and masculine grandeur, as well as with its nobleness in the wild. Unlike other large cats, it does not try to conceal itself in cover but promenades in the open in a secure and apparently fearless manner. Egyptians, Greeks, and Romans were equally fascinated with the lion's aesthetic and romantic majesty and used him as a symbol of such.

PA: Used as an emblem of courage, ferocity, and strength by European kings on coats of arms and by knights on their shields. Richard the Lion-Hearted was the first king of England to have three lions on the shield of the royal coat of arms. The male, though elegant and imposing with his large mane, is lazy and allows the females to do his hunting (lazy or smart?). Though lions are the only social breed of cat, traveling and living in prides, the male will as easily kill young kittens as he will tolerate their play with him. If neutered, a young male lion will never develop a mane. Of all human-lion relationships, obviously that of Joy Adamson and Elsa is the most famous. Other persons, such as Ron Whitfield, also have very special bonds with these big cats.

Page 15
Asian Lion: *Panthera Leo Persica*

Characteristics: weight three hundred to four hundred pounds; head and body length eight to nine feet; tail two to three feet

Habitat: bush, woodlands

Habits: hunts by day and night; terrestrial and territorial

Prey: mostly hoofed animals and some large birds

Distribution: Once much of Asia; today only a 450-mile-square reserve in the Gir Forest in northwest India

Longevity: ten to twelve years in the wild; twenty years or more in captivity

Comments: Believed to be slight of mane; however, captive-raised animals are just as hairy as African lions. Because of their small population in the wild, where less than two hundred of these animals survive, large-maned lions are probably scarce; most have been eliminated by trophy hunters. While Asian lions are endangered in the wild, there is now a surplus of them in captivity, which makes it almost impossible to find homes for captive-bred cubs. Thus, most zoos fit their lionesses with contraceptive devices to prevent pregnancy.

Pages 16 and 17

Cheetah: *Acinonyx Jubatus*

Characteristics: weight eighty-five to one hundred forty pounds; head and body length four to five feet; tail twenty to thirty inches

Habitat: acacia, scrub, plains, light woodland, semidesert

Habits: terrestrial; hunts during day

Prey: small antelope, other ungulates, hares

Distribution: Africa, southern Asia

Comments: Second only to the domestic cat in its historical association with man, cheetahs were trained for hunting by the ancient Egyptians, and until the early part of this century by maharajahs in India. Over short distance they have been timed at 70 mph (112 kph), though about 50 mph (80 kph) is more usual. Cheetahs also have an extraordinarily fast acceleration, taking merely seconds from a resting position to achieve a speed of 40 mph (64 kph), which is as rapid as—if not more so than—the average sports car.

PA: Seemingly the most tractable of all wild cats. There are stories of adult cheetahs being captured in the wild and later relatively easily trained.

Pages 18 and 19

Sumatran Tigress: *Panthera Tigris sumatrae*

Comments: As the tigress lunges at an intruder (me and my camera), her face is distorted into the ferocious expression that taxidermists try to give to feline trophies. This also is the look that strikes fear into any heart when imagining what it must have been like in a man-eating tiger's territory in India a half century or more ago. Few villagers had firearms except some primitive single-shot weapons held together with wire.

On the subject of man-eating tigers, Jim Corbett tells us: "A man-eating tiger is a tiger that has been compelled through stress of circumstances beyond its control, to adopt a diet alien to it. The stress of circumstances is, in nine cases out of ten, wounds, and in the tenth case old age. The wound that has caused a particular tiger to take to man-eating might be the result of a carelessly fired shot and the failure to follow up and recover the wounded animal, or be the result of the tiger having lost his temper when killing a porcupine. Human beings are not the natural prey of tigers, and it is only when tigers have been incapacitated through wounds or old age, in order to live, they are compelled to take to a diet of human flesh."

Pages 22 and 23

Cat Touching Man's Fingers at Campfire: *Felis Catus*

Comments: Before becoming domesticated, the cat lived like any other wild feline, by its cunning and extraordinary hunting ability. Not until the third millennium B.C., long after the dog had been domesticated, did the cat concede and accept the hand and companionship of man.

Pages 24 and 25

Lynx-point Shorthair: *Felis Catus*

Comments: In ancient Egypt house cats were adorned with jeweled collars, and pendants from silver, bronze, and gold chains were hung about their necks. Sometimes the ears of the cat would be pierced in preparation for the wearing of gold earrings or jeweled studs. Owners of domestic felines lavished affection on their animals, and sick cats were treated with the care reserved for ailing children—no cost was spared in trying to obtain medicines and potions to effect a cure. Their food was cut into small pieces to prevent them from choking on it, and they were frequently encouraged to eat off their masters' plates. Feasts of bread soaked in milk were even offered to strays. In turn, the cats kept the Egyptian households free of snakes, rats, and mice.

Jean Cantin tells us that in Egypt "cats also had something to do with the healing of the sick, though their roles in this service was indirect at best. When the child of a wealthy Egyptian became seriously ill, the family wasted no time in seeking the help of Bastet (the cat goddess). All the relatives of the child immediately shaved the hair off their heads and sold it for gold or silver. The money was delivered to the temple and used by the keeper to purchase milk and fish for the cats held there for the sole purpose of worship. The family gathered in the temple, and while the priests chanted, the cats devoured the food. The relatives of the sick child found great significance in looking into the eyes of the cats and determining from their strange gaze whether or not the child would recover."

Pages 26 and 27

Tiger Cub: *Panthera Tigris*

PA: Persons who work with tigers say that you have to try very hard to make one mean—because of their great size they feel relatively unthreatened and tend generally to be rather mellow in captivity. All cats change to some degree when they reach sexual maturity, becoming more aggressive, solitary, and so on. The males also begin to spray, marking their territories. Females of most species also spray but to a lesser degree, primarily when coming into and during estrus. Some cats will go

173

through a period of change at the beginning of sexual maturity, then become more mellow as they grow older.

Page 28
Tabby Short-haired Kitten: *Felis Catus*

Comments: Angela Sayer tells us: "Though the brain of the young kitten is functional at birth, its intelligence depends to a large extent on the number of synaptic junctions that form during the first few weeks of life. Proper stimuli and slight amounts of stress during the first critical weeks appear to help development of the brain and so produce more clever cats.

"Experiments have been conducted where litters were split, half being kept as a control and left to lead a normal life in their nest box until weaning time, the other half insistently stressed by extra handling and subjection to sounds, smells, and sights. In all cases the stressed kittens matured to surpass their littermates in intelligence, calm acceptance of handling by strangers, and resistance to nervous disorders.

"In normal rearing practice, the kittens should be frequently handled between the ages of four and eight weeks. This period is equivalent to the nest-changing in the wild and is the time for young kittens to recognize the difference between safety and danger."

Page 30
Canadian Lynx: *Felis Lynx Canadensis*

Characteristics: weight thirty to thirty-five pounds; head and body length about forty inches; tail about seven inches

Habitat: pine forest, thick scrub

Habits: generally hunts at night on the ground

Prey: rabbits and hares, rodents, fish, birds, deer, and other domestic animals

Distribution: Canada and northern United States

Comments: This lynx has not been declawed or defanged like many exotic felines kept as pets. Often more harmful than a big cat's teeth are its claws, especially the hind ones. While the cat grasps its prey's neck and shoulders with its mouth and the claws of its front legs, it often digs with its hind-leg claws to disembowel the victim.

PA: If a captive cat is declawed, there may be a problem placing him with another cat that does have claws. The declawed cat will continue to go through the ritual of "sharpening his claws" on stumps or a piece of wood. Felines in captivity also go through the instinctive motion of "digging" a hole (even if they are housed on cement or wood) prior to defecating, then afterward scratch as if to cover the feces even if there is not dirt or other matter available. They will do the same when they've had enough to eat, scratching with their front paws as if to cover the food container. In captivity many will also defecate in their water bowl—since in the wild they frequently defecate in water to hide their scent from other predators. Contrary to what most books say about their behavior in the wild, in captivity lynxes are vocal year round, more so during breeding season. They have a wide range of sounds like most cats.

other humans who accompany their owners into the cage to handle the kittens. With the exception of the domestic cat, which humans have carried to all parts of the globe, only one of the thirty-six species of cat is common to both the Old World and the New: the lynx.

Page 31
Canadian Lynx: *Felis Lynx Canadensis*

Comments: This female lynx, who here freezes so that she appears to be stuffed, has raised several litters of cubs in captivity. Whereas in the wild a female will become fiercely protective of her young, in captivity usually a hand-raised cat will not object to the presence of "her humans" while she is giving birth or to their handling the cubs while she is still nursing and caring for them.

PA: Our female cougar, Chirpa, likes me to be with her when she's delivering and loves people sitting with her, handling her babies while she cares for them. She purrs and licks your arm and dotes on the attention, often reaching out with a big furry paw around your ankle if you attempt to leave. The bobcat and Siberian lynx do the same, as would other feline females if they were tame. The female bobcat actually carries her babies out of the den box to show visitors, and if I put them back in the box and we start to leave, she calls to us and starts bringing them out again. The trust that these cats have seems to enable them to trust

Pages 32 and 33
Oriental Pointed Shorthair: *Felis Catus*

Comments: The Oriental or foreign shorthair is a cat that resembles a Siamese in shape but not in color. By 1000 B.C. cats were well known in China, and from there spread to Japan and probably India—though some evidence suggests that the domestication of cats there had begun as early as it had in Egypt. In Japan cats were regarded as so precious that they were always kept on leads, until A.D. 1602, when the government ordered their release so they could deal more effectively with vermin that threatened the silk industry. The Japanese used to believe that the cat had power to cure fits, epilepsy, and melancholy. It has been said that "an affectionate, playful cat is the best specific ever invented against melancholy."

Page 34
Abyssinian Kittens: *Felis Catus*

Comments: The Abyssinian has also been called the "rabbit" or the "bunny" cat, because its fur is ticked, that is, each individual hair shows light and dark coloration. This cat has such great visual appeal, both in its physique and in the fact that it looks like a "little wild feline," that even persons who are really not that keen on domestic cats often confess, "Well, if I ever had a cat, it would be one of those."

Pages 36 and 37
Black Leopard: *Panthera Pardus*

Comments: Incorrectly and frequently called "black panther." Does have spots that can be seen in bright light.

PA: It can't be emphasized too much that wild felines in captivity never lose their wild instincts. Perhaps the best-known breeder and handler of leopards in America had a mature male that he had raised from birth, and their relationship was quite exceptional, considering the general unpredictability of leopards. For a period of several days the man cut to practically nothing the cat's meal ration in preparation for training it, at the sound of a buzzer, to cross from Point A to B, after which, having reached his destination, he would be rewarded with food. (This sort of buzzer training enables animals to be worked off a leash for movies, TV commercials, and so forth.) One day the trainer, whom all animal people respected as knowing more about leopards than any human being, was found dead, killed by the leopard in its cage. Eighteen pounds of flesh had been eaten from the trainer's upper body. When the man on the street suddenly is overcome with the desire to adopt a lion, tiger, or leopard cub, he should remember that the trainer from this story wasn't just another cat person—he was one of the best, with years of knowledge and experience.

There are many documented accounts such as the above, relating how "tame" cats seemingly "reverted." In most of these instances the attacks were caused because the cats were suffering from serious illness. For example, a friend of ours had a very tame bobcat. One day the woman went into the cat's cage for the usual play ritual and the cat lunged at her face, ripping it to pieces. She was only able to get away by strangling the cat into temporary unconsciousness. The woman had to have thirty-seven stitches in her face. Later, a necropsy revealed that the bobcat had been suffering from severe liver damage. We were told of this same thing happening with a tiger and also with a cougar—and I'm sure it's happened with every breed of cat.

Pages 38 and 39
White Shorthair: *Felis Catus*

Comments: As in the long-haired breeds, the white shorthair may also show the odd-eyed syndrome, in this case one blue and one yellow eye. Since blue-eyed white cats are frequently deaf, it has been said that by giving the cat eyes of two different colors, nature prevents hearing problems.

In France it is a custom that at harvest time a cat is decorated with ribbons, flowers, and cornstalks, first at the start of the reaping and then at the end of the harvest. This would seem a symbolic form of sacrifice to the goddess of harvest, since the cat is so closely associated with fertility and fertility goddesses. Cats have long been popular with the French, some of whom have not only bestowed great affection, but also gifts upon their pets. In the seventeenth century a famous harpist there, Mme. Dupuis, included this clause in her will: "Item 1, I desire my sister, Marie Bluteau, and my niece Madame Calonge, to look after my cats. If both cats should survive me, thirty sous a week must be laid out upon them, in order that they may live well. They are to be served daily, in a clean and proper manner, . . . with two meals of meat soup, the same as we eat ourselves, but it is to be given them in two soup plates. The bread is not to be cut up into the soup, but must be broken into squares about the size of a nut, otherwise they will refuse to eat it. A ration of meat, finely minced, is to be added to it; the whole is then to be mildly seasoned, put into a clean pan, covered close, and carefully simmered before it is dished up. If only one cat should survive, half the mention will suffice."

Page 41
Cheetah: *Acinonyx Jubatus*

Comments: PA: Contrary to the general feeling that caging wild felines is cruel, a cat born in captivity who knows only cage life becomes very content and secure—if he is *properly* housed—with his surroundings, and usually shows no desire to leave his cage if given the opportunity. A cat that has been caught wild, however, is another story and usually paces frantically or hides and almost always remains in a state of stress. Cats, being highly intelligent, in captivity need stimulation to keep their minds and bodies active, toys to play with, trees to climb, and so forth. Osa Johnson had a young cheetah or two that she brought back from safari to her home in Nairobi, where the animals lived in the house and in the garden. Joy Adamson was first introduced to the hand-raised cheetah Pippa, sitting on a chair at a table in the New Stanley Hotel, having tea with its owners. Pippa was the subject of Joy's book *Spotted Sphinx.* Later Joy taught Pippa to fend for herself and released her, as she had done with Elsa, into the wild, where Pippa eventually mated and led Joy to her first litter of cubs. Arthur, the Marine World–Africa USA cheetah, though a mature cat, still has a deep affection for his babyhood stuffed animal, "Mr. Lion." We helped on a recent TV commercial in which Arthur was let loose on a forty-thousand-acre piece of wild habitat and required to run at top speed toward the camera. This was accomplished by using Mr. Lion as a lure. Arthur would run for the stuffed toy when it was taken from him and not stop until he had reached it.

Page 42
Marmalade Shorthair: *Felis Catus*

Comments: Perhaps the most famous marmalade cat of all time was Morris, about whom my friend Mary Daniels wrote a biography. Mary describes the morning that she and the famous star of feline-food television commercials appeared on NBC's *Today* show: "A few minutes later we 'cat people' were ushered into the studio. It was a huge, dark vault with the brightly lighted *Today* desk at the back and swirls of rubber coils, props, and cameras all about.

"'Where's a mike for Morris? Have you got a mike for Morris?' Shalit demanded, as crew people clipped them on the rest of us.

"'We have only twenty seconds,' a crew member warned. 'Put a mike on him!' Shalit ordered.

"'Ten seconds,' someone said. A pretty girl slipped a mike around Morris's neck; he was sitting in a director's chair, his name stenciled across the back.

"'Two seconds,' said the voice. The girl took her hands away.

"Then we were on, with Shalit first telling of Morris's stature and success; then switching to ask Martwick how to choose a cat at a shelter (which is how Morris was discovered). I stole a look at the distinguished subject and almost laughed aloud. Just as Martwick was saying, 'Well, don't pick a cat that just lies there and doesn't do anything,' Morris was slowly sinking into his resting place in a half-snooze.

"It was all over quickly. As we left the building, a wave of people fussed over Morris (who mysteriously became very alert again).

"Later, talking to Martwick, I asked after Morris, who lives at Martwick's country kennels near Chicago. 'Do you still think . . .' I began and Martwick finished for me, 'that he's the greatest cat who ever lived?'

"'Yes,' he said, then chuckled and added, 'and so does he.'"

Page 45
Abyssinian Cat: *Felis Catus*

Comments: It has been speculated that the Abyssinian is the oldest breed of foreign shorthair. Because mummified remains of cats from ancient Egypt have the color particular to the Abyssinian, it is often assumed that they were the cats of the Pharaohs. However, blue and black cats were also kept by the Egyptians. Another theory states that the Abyssinian was once a prized possession in

Ethiopia, where it was known as the "desert cat" because of its coat. However, the origin of the Abyssinian is still a controversial subject. What *is* true is that it is a fascinating and beautiful little cat.

Although the Pharaohs held sacred fish, cows, and serpents, the most divine of the creatures they worshiped was the cat, or *mau*. The reverence and concern for the well-being of domestic felines was passed on from father to son. When one of these sacred cats died, it was embalmed and the owners grieved as though they had lost a human family member. Wealthy families had ornate sarcophaguses made for their dead pets, and embalmed mice were placed next to the cat for future meals. In ancient Egypt the cat undoubtedly enjoyed the most refined, calm, and serene conditions that any civilization would ever offer it.

In Egypt in 1890 over three million cat mummies were uncovered still enclosed in their cases of engraved wood or wrapped in colored, intertwined straw and bound in rich stripes of brightly colored fabrics. Covering the dead felines' faces were masks on which the nose, eyes, ears, and whiskers had been painted and carved.

Page 46

Black-and-White Long-haired Kitten: *Felis Catus*

Comments: Black-and-white cats are called "magpies" by breeders and showers. Carl Burton comments, "Cats, kittens and little girls go together, too, and this is about as sentimental as the Victorians ever got about their cats. Even Lewis Carroll's Alice loses some of her charm when she scolds her cat. Cats make good mothers. They are clean and loving and, at the same time, thoroughgoing disciplinarians. Thus they furnish lovely role models for little Victorian girls who have only one career to look forward to: Marriage and all that entails. Mothering kittens, like mothering dolls, provides good practice." The nursery rhyme that is reproduced with this photograph is, perhaps, except for "the three little kittens who lost their mittens," one of the most famous pieces of cat literature. Cats have long been both friends and subjects of such literary figures as Baudelaire, the Brontë sisters, Lord Byron, Jean Cocteau, Colette, Confucius, Charles Dickens, T. S. Eliot, Anatole France, Paul Gallico, Thomas Hardy, Ernest Hemingway, Victor Hugo, Henry James, Guy de Maupassant, Edgar Allan Poe, Sir Walter Scott, George Bernard Shaw, Mark Twain, H. G. Wells, William Wordsworth, W. B. Yeats, and Emile Zola.

Pages 48 and 49
African Lion Cubs: *Panthera leo*

Comments: African lion cubs are among the most appealing of all baby animals, which is partly responsible for many of them being bought by humans for pets. However, the majority of these animals, once they become too large and strong to be easily controlled, change owners until they must eventually be destroyed.

PA: Exotic cats can never be pets in the fireside-tabby sense of the word. The best feline companion for humans, in which all of the grace and hunting behavior of the lion or tiger may be seen, is the domestic cat. Even though exotic cats are born in captivity, there will always remain something of the wild animal in them. Only in breeding, educational, or behavioral-study programs should exotic cats be kept in captivity—except in our imaginations. Most people simply do not have the psychological or economic resources to keep wild cats in even minimally humane conditions. Of great importance, however, is that those felines that are or may become endangered be maintained in captive-breeding programs. If in these breeding programs the cats have friendly relationships with their human companions, this makes such an endeavor even more enjoyable for both feline and human.

(PA in a letter that accompanied her notes for this book): I didn't want to get into what a spine-tingling, fabulous experience it is to develop a relationship, as we have, with these potentially dangerous cats and to be accepted by them as a friend. The dream of being involved in such a situation is what makes so many people want to have a lion or a cheetah or a cougar in spite of the drawbacks. And these persons, usually with good intentions, but without the capacity to handle such a situation, always say, "Oh, no *mine* [my cat] will be different." They make the remark in the same way as they do when they are planning to have children and are told about problems today with drug abuse and the like. But with the cats there is *always* the realization that they are, first and foremost, a *wild animal* with all those instincts for hunting and killing, and so forth. They can be trained to a certain degree, but *never*, fortunately, domesticated—and that is their beauty and intrigue and challenge.

Pages 50 and 51
American Silver Short-haired Tabby: *Felis Catus*

Comments: The silver is one of three short-haired varieties, the others being brown and red. Classic tabby markings include rings on the tail and spots on the abdomen. The word *tabby* may come from the Turkish name *Attabiya*, the quarter of Baghdad where, in the twelfth century, watered silk was manufactured. The cat's stripes are similar to the *moiré* pattern of fabric.

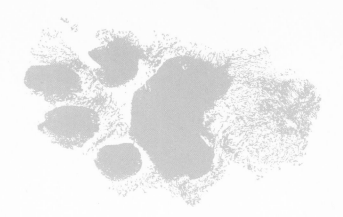

Pages 52 and 53
Temminck's Golden Cat: *Felis Temmincki*

Characteristics: weight fourteen to twenty-five pounds; head and body length thirty-one to thirty-five inches; tail nineteen to twenty inches
Habitat: forest interspersed with rocky terrain
Habits: probably diurnal, mainly terrestrial
Prey: all types of birds and rodents, and other small mammals up to the size of small deer
Distribution: Himalayas to Southeast Asia
Comments: Rare in captivity. The animal in this photograph was friendly with women and would allow them to caress him, but extremely apprehensive of men, seeming on the verge of attacking any human male who approached. It took some time before I was able to get close enough to photograph him.

Page 54
Bicolor Shorthair: *Felis Catus*

Comments: "A kitten is more amusing than half the people one is obliged to be with," once remarked Lady Sydney Morgan, one of the many humans who prefer feline company to that of people. George Balanchine, the choreographer, said on a number of occasions that he also preferred cats to people, and even taught his cat Mourka to execute *jetés* and *tours en l'air*, classical ballet leaps and turns. An autobiography of Mourka was written by Balanchine's dancer wife, Tanaquil LeClercq. It is reported that once, as Balanchine gazed at Mourka, he joyfully exclaimed, "At last a body worth choreographing for!"

Pages 56 and 57
Oncillas: *Leopardus Tigrinus*

Characteristics: weight four to six pounds; head and body length twenty-one inches; tail length thirteen inches
Habitat: forests
Habits: very little known
Distribution: Costa Rica to northern Argentina
Comments: Appear almost as miniature ocelots, except that their body lines are more elegant and their eyes not as large, dark, and mascaraed. One of the most difficult felines to domesticate.

PA: In captivity, all cats, with the exception of the very small ones (oncilla, leopard cat, and so forth), can be easily tamed and trained if taken from their mothers early enough by a person who has the knowledge, common sense, and sensitivity to do so. They can all be taught to walk reasonably well on a leash or chain. The smaller cats are much more highly strung, easily stressed, and generally afraid of and aggressive toward people than the larger ones are. They seem to feel threatened by everything and everybody, whereas, because of their large size, the larger cats are more mellow in temperament—they don't possess those fears and threats. The oncilla is closely related to and often mistaken for the margay and geoffroys cat. Breeds well in captivity with male sometimes aggressive toward female.

Pages 58 and 59
Black Persian: *Felis Catus*

Comments: It is said that Charles I of England had a black cat, which he carried with him wherever he went, commenting that the cat brought him good luck. When the cat died the king lamented, "Now my luck is gone." The following day the king was arrested and later beheaded by Oliver Cromwell. On the other hand, a cat—black or not—crossing one's path was considered bad luck as long ago as ancient Greece, and was mentioned by both Aristophanes and Theophrastus.

Pages 60 and 61
Bengal Tiger: *Panthera Tigris Tigris*

Comments: While tigers in the wild live solitary lives except after pairing during the mating season, in captivity, where they no longer have to compete for food and territory, pairs form strong bonds and enjoy each other's companionship. In India, not only do maharajahs have a history of hunting tigers and sometimes keeping them for pets, but millions of households have domestic cats. The Hindu religion states that the housing and feeding of one domestic cat is theoretically demanded of all the faithful. The so-called law of Manu dictates that "He who has killed a cat must withdraw to the middle forest and there dedicate himself to the life of the animals around him until he is purified."

Pages 62 and 63
Siamese: *Felis Catus*

Comments: It is generally agreed that this, the most popular of all purebred cats, has its origin in Thailand. The first recorded pair of Siamese in the Western world were imported in 1884 into England by the British consul general in Bangkok. These cats were exhibited at the Crystal Palace in London in 1885. Until then solely the royalty of Siam could breed Siamese cats—for more than two centuries they could be encountered only in the court gardens of Bangkok, where they were fed the best of food and housed in gold cages perfumed with burning incense. Upon the death of a member of the royal family, a live cat was placed in the tomb. However, a small hole was made in the roof and if the cat found his way out through it, it was thought that the soul of the dead person had transcended, and the cat was honorably moved through the temple. Some Siamese cats have two

darker markings on either side of their necks. Called "the temple marks," these dark markings are felt to be the fingerprints of God, who is said to have picked the cat up by the scruff of the neck. Siamese warriors reportedly trained cats to sit on their shoulders so that the animals could alert them with warning cries when an enemy approached.

Siamese cats were first introduced into the United States about 1840, and were reported to have been a gift from the king of Siam to an American friend.

The blue eyes of the Siamese result from a low distribution of melanin in the iris. This lack of pigmentation behind the retina causes the Siamese's eyes to reflect red instead of green in the dark.

possess characteristics of each. Being arboreal in their native habitat, they are extremely agile and adept at climbing, balancing, hanging by one paw from great heights. From birth they possess a much greater degree of coordination than other cats do. Their canine teeth are larger in relationship to their skull than any other cat, and they are thought to be the feline most directly related to the saber-toothed tiger. Because of the length of these canines, their jaws—to accommodate their teeth—open wider than those of other cats. These tusks are highly prized by the natives of Borneo, who use them for decoration and will pay high prices for them. They also use the leopards' pelts for seat mats, and skins were sold in Europe to fashion "booties" to be worn over boots and shoes.

Pages 64 and 65
Clouded Leopard: *Neofelis Nebulosa*

Characteristics: weight forty-five pounds; head and body length thirty inches; tail thirty inches
Habitat: dense forest
Habits: primarily a tree dweller, leaps onto prey from branches
Prey: large birds, monkeys, rodents, deer, goats
Distribution: southern Asia, Borneo, Sumatra
Comments: PA: Though classified as a large cat, they are smaller than the cougar, which is listed as a small cat. The cloudeds are said to be the bridge between the large and small cats as they

Pages 66 and 67
Diluted Calico Shorthair: *Felis Catus*

Comments: Of the many creation myths, one relates that "When God created the world, He chose to inhabit it with animals, and decided to give each whatever it wanted. Before His throne all the animals formed a long line. He gave strength to the elephant and the bear; swiftness to the deer and rabbit; the ability to see at night to the owl; great beauty to birds and butterflies; cunning to the fox; intelligence to the monkey; loyalty to the dog; courage to the lion; playfulness to the otter. And these were the things that all the animals begged of God. When at last He came to the end of the line, there sat a small cat, patiently waiting.

"'And just what do you want?' God asked the cat.

"Shrugging modestly, the cat replied, 'Oh, whatever scraps you have left over. I'm not particular.'

"'But I am God. I have *everything* left over.'

"'Then I'll have a little of that, please.'

"And God shouted with joy at the cleverness of such a small animal, and gave the cat everything she asked for, adding grace and elegance and, only for her, a gentle purr that was sure to attract humans and forever assure her a warm and comfortable home.

"But he took away her false modesty."

Pages 68 and 69
Serval: *Felis Serval*

Characteristics: weight thirty-five pounds; head and body thirty-two inches; tail sixteen inches

Habitat: generally near water with heavy cover of reeds, scrub, or high grass

Habits: nocturnal, but if hungry will hunt in daylight; terrestrial

Prey: rats, small birds, lizards, young or small antelope

Distribution: Algeria, Africa south of the Sahara

Comments: PA: Called the "poor man's cheetah" because of the similarity in markings and their somewhat disproportionate body, long legs, and small head. South African natives call them the "bush cat" because of their preference for thick bush country over open plains. In captivity they breed throughout the year, often having three litters per year. Swift and agile in their movements, they hunt much like the fox, cocking their ear to the ground, then leaping up in the air and coming down on their prey or down with a front leg in a mole or gopher hole. Ours often do this when we take them out on thirty-foot lunge lines.

Pages 70 and 71
White Tigress: *Panthera Tigris*

Comments: Except on her tail, this tigress lacks body stripes. Wild felines, like this female, that are born and hand-raised in captivity bond strongly not only to their human companions, but also to their feline mates.

PA: Our pairs are almost always curled up together, often will eat from the same bowl, never fight over food, play together, and show great displays of affection (i.e., licking, grooming, wanting to be close to one another). In captivity, without the competition for food, territory, mates, and so forth that these cats encounter in the wild, there is no threat. Macho, our male cougar, will stand in his cage and cry when we take his mate, Chirpa, out for a walk. When she is returned to him they greet each other with a head rub or soft butt, chirp, and also affectionately lick one another. Our other species of cats use the same greeting ritual, even if they've only been separated (and not out of sight of one another) for a short time. All of our tame females want the males within sight and hearing when they're separated to give birth and raise their babies. If a male is out of range, the female becomes restless and sometimes will not care for her young.

Pages 72 and 73
White Tiger: *Panthera Tigris*

Comments: PA: When you first told me of plans for this book, the idea of photographing cats adorned as they were ornamented at times in history was an idea that I didn't know if I could accept, since a great part of the cats' appeal to me had always been their natural elegance and beauty. However, upon looking at this photograph of the white tiger adorned with jewelry, it seems to me that you have again created some kind of magic with elegant fantasy.

Of course, adorning cats, wild and domestic, with ornaments is a thing of the past, something that, until your photographs, has lived only in paintings and in our imaginations. These images are wonderfully romantic in the tradition of Delacroix and Rousseau, combining the natural beauty of nature with artistic sensibility. As with your unicorn book, once more you have proved the right to adorn felines as they were adorned in ancient civilizations and to further the acceptance of

photography not simply as representing documentary realism but as an art in which only the artist's imagination provides limitations.

Page 74
Abyssinian: *Felis Catus*

Comments: Part of this cat's charm is that it appears to look less like a domestic cat than other breeds. It almost suggests a miniature mountain lion.

PA: Ours, Chester, lived both inside and outside, hunting daily for his food and wandering far afield, yet coming home every night to be inside and pampered. If he arrived home after we were in bed he would strum our window screen like someone plucking a stringed instrument and yowl loudly until we let him in. Inside he wanted to be a lap cat, purring and kneading with his paws.

Page 77
Black Shorthair: *Felis Catus*

Comments: A cat's eyes do not glow in the dark because of moonshine or sunshine but because of their *tapetum lucidum* membrane that reflects light. The cat is aided by its slit pupil, which is very sensitive to ultraviolet light. Since cats hunt at night, until recently it was thought that they were color-blind; however, it has been found

that they can perceive and be conditioned to distinguish between a limited range of color, differentiating red and blue from each other and from white. Green, yellow, and white, however, all probably appear similar, and red is seen as dark gray.

An old Chinese legend relates: "Someone has said that the pupil of the cat's eyes marks the time: at midnight, noon, sunrise, and sunset, it is like a thread; at four o'clock and ten o'clock morning and evening, it is round like a full moon; while at two o'clock and eight o'clock, morning and evening, it is elliptical like the kernel of a date." Like the Chinese, some Africans and other peoples believe that one can tell time by looking at a cat's eyes—the pupil is wide in the morning, narrow vertical at noon, and broader again in the later afternoon.

Page 78
Scottish Wildcat: *Felis Sylvestris Grampia*

Characteristics: weight ten to thirty pounds; head and body length twenty-two to twenty-eight inches; tail length about twelve inches

Habitat: woodland and high rocky terrain, occasionally on heathland, moors, and marshes

Habits: mainly crepuscular; also hunts at dawn

Prey: small rodents, squirrels, rabbits, birds— wild and domestic—young deer, small animals

Distribution: Scotland

Comments: It has been hypothesized that the European wildcat, along with the African wildcat and Pallas cat, are the ancestors of the domestic cat. The European wildcat has a reputation of being extremely difficult to tame.

PA: The most quoted line on this breed is that though little is known of them in their natural habitat, "naturalists and wildlife biologists agree that they are completely untamable." Our Scottish wildcat, MacDuff, never read that book. Taken from his mother and hand-raised, he is today, as an adult, heavily imprinted on me, wanting to spend all his time purring, rubbing against me, and snuggling up to me.

Pages 80 and 81
Sphynx Kittens: *Felis Catus*

Comments: Also known as moon cats, *chats sans poil* (cats without hair). Said to closely resemble the Mexican Hairless. The hairless cat is a mutation, the result of breeding two normal cats who carry the hairless recessive gene. First reaction upon seeing one is commonly, "It looks like E.T." Hairless kittens are said to bond more rapidly and firmly to humans because the familiar hairless skin of their mothers is similar in feeling to our own. Not having hair around their eyes makes their stares appear harder and strikes some people as evil.

This evilness was attributed to all cats during

the Middle Ages in Europe, when they were viewed as sinister and linked with Satan. The cat's important role in pagan festivals, together with its independent and nocturnal habits, condemned it not only as a symbol of evil but to being roasted alive, flayed, disemboweled, and tortured in hundreds of fiendish ways. In fact, so many cats were killed that the rat population multiplied tremendously, leading to the great bubonic plague, or Black Death, in 1348, which decimated Europe. Ironically, during the plague a cat was worth its weight in gold.

Page 82
Orange Tabby Longhair: *Felis Catus*

Comments: In the low foothills of coastal California, a mountain lion slowly lifts a paw as it silently stalks a mule deer. On a nearby ranch, a common domestic cat slowly lifts a paw and stalks a gopher. Cats of the world—large or small, spotted or striped, orange or black—practically mirror each other's behavior patterns. They are all members of an ancient family of hunters.

As the cat in this photograph sits, it purrs. Kenneth Anderson comments: "One of the longstanding mysteries of the cat is to make purring noises. Cats of all species purr when they are contented, although the purring sound can also occur when they are in pain. Biologists have determined that purring does not originate in the larynx (voice box). One prevalent theory is that it is generated by

vibrations in the chest of the cat which are brought on by increased activity in major blood vessels there. But ultimately, the origin and function of the purr remains unexplained."

Pages 84 and 85
Snow Leopard: *Felis Uncia*

Characteristics: weight one hundred to one hundred fifty pounds; head and body length about forty-one inches; tail length about thirty-five inches

Habitat: high mountains above tree line

Habits: hunts during day on ground

Prey: large birds, hoofed wild and domestic animals, marmots, pikas

Distribution: Kashmir, Tibet, Himalayas

Longevity: little known; estimated at more than ten years in captivity

Comments: Until recently seldom studied in the wild. Not long ago the subject of observation by George Schaller, accompanied by Peter Matthiessen, who later wrote the book *The Snow Leopard*. Population for the entire Himalayan region is estimated at between two hundred and six hundred individuals. The Bronx Zoo of New York has at least half a dozen of them in their breeding program, and many other zoos have active breeding programs. In captivity they are successful breeders that have been found to possess a milder disposition than the spotted leopards.

Domestic Cats with Nuns: *Felis Catus*

Comments: In the Middle Ages, nunneries had this rule: "Ye my sisters, shall have no beast but a cat." Christianity has expressed both love and hate for cats. It was written of Pope Gregory the Great that "his greatest pleasure came from stroking his cat." Cardinal Richelieu's passion for cats was such that "when he rose in the morning and went to bed at night he was always surrounded by dozens of them. . . . He had one of his chambers fitted as a cattery." All fourteen of Richelieu's cats were waited on by servants and fed on chicken breasts cooked into a pâté. Henry VIII's minister Cardinal Wolsey carried his cat with him to state functions, which caused one foreign diplomat in a letter home to comment that nothing like it had been seen since Caligula made his horse a consul in Rome. The cat, however, is the only domestic animal not mentioned in the Bible.

Clouded Leopard: *Neofelis Nebulosa*

Characteristics: weight forty-five pounds; head and body length thirty inches; tail thirty inches

Habitat: dense forest

Habits: primarily a tree dweller, leaps onto prey from branches

Prey: large birds, monkeys, rodents, deer, goats

Distribution: southern Asia, Borneo, Sumatra

Comments: PA: Clouded leopards are called "the little saber-toothed tigers of the trees," and "mint leopards," because their rosettes are the shape of the mint leaf in their native country. Their pelts are probably the most striking of all cats and combine the rosettes of a jaguar, the spots of a leopard, and the stripes of a tiger. Unlike most other exotic cats, with clouded leopards in captivity there is a great tendency for males to kill the females during breeding and also for the mother to cannibalize her young. It would appear that they mate for life in the wild. In captivity it has been found that chances for successful breeding are enhanced by raising young pairs together and allowing them to bond prior to sexual maturity. This has certainly been true in our case, and our male is extremely gentle during breeding. A female also proved to be a perfect mother with her first litter.

Brown Tabby Persian: *Felis Catus*

Comments: The brown tabby is the oldest variety of this breed; although very popular during the last century, it is now relatively rare.

Page 93
Cheetah: *Acinonyx Jubatus*

Comments: PA: Cats that are caged together in groups instead of alone are never as dependent on the humans who raised them as they would be if they were isolated and relied only on human companionship. Hand-raised cats, as they mature, will frequently show a strong sexual preference to humans (i.e., female cats prefer men and male cats women). Unlike some other species (primarily birds), cats that have a strong bonding with a human will, nonetheless, bond with their own species and breed and produce young successfully. I feel that the hand-raised cats, in many situations, make better breeders because they're not as stressed as ones caught wild. Having the mother tame also allows us to save sick kittens and care for them properly. Our tame mothers will allow us to check to make sure they have an adequate milk supply and that their babies are all right. Because we can handle them, hand-raised cats can be checked periodically for health problems, given shots, and otherwise medicated. Cats, being predators, often mask all signs of illness. Therefore, in many cases, by the time they appear weak or ill it is often too late to save them. All of our cats have their litter boxes cleaned every day, since changes in color and density of urine or feces are a first indication of illness. Although it was long believed, and written many times, that a cheetah's claws, unlike those of every other member of the cat family, were not retractable, in truth, they are.

But they lack the sheath that every other kind of cat possesses, and so it appears at first glance that they don't retract.

Pages 94 and 95
Russian Blue: *Felis Catus*

Comments: Sailors and travelers who visited Russia first imported these cats to the rest of Europe, though it is said that they were also prevalent in Scandinavian countries. Commenting on the cat in Europe over the years, and the independent ways that led to its being used as a symbol of freedom, Louise Caldi tells us: "This face [independence] did not escape the ancient Romans who were responsible for introducing the cat into many areas of Europe during their conquest. A cat was represented at the feet of the great statue of the Goddess of Liberty in Rome, and cats were emblazoned upon shields and flags of Roman soldiers as symbols of independence. Throughout history the cat has reappeared as a symbol of freedom. It was used on the coat of arms of the early Dukes of Burgundy and by the Burgundian wife of Clovis, the fifth-century Frankish king. In their struggle for liberation during the sixteenth century, the Dutch used the cat as a sign of independence, as did the French two centuries later duiring their own revolution."

Page 96
Caracal Lynx: *Felis Caracal*

Characteristics: weight up to fifty pounds; head and body length twenty-eight inches; tail nine inches

Habitat: savannah, scrub, desert, mountain ranges

Habits: primarily nocturnal, hunts on ground but is an excellent jumper and climber

Prey: small and large birds, rodents, fawns, small antelope

Distribution: Africa and Asia

Comments: PA: One of the few wild cats, besides the cheetah, that has a historical relationship with man, having been tamed in India and trained there as a hunter. Explorer and photographer Armand Denis, while living in Nairobi, had a pet caracal that was very affectionate. Sometimes, however, the cat would become possessive and start growling and acting ferocious, at which point Denis would place a saucer of milk before it, and it would immediately begin to lap it up and once more start purring and behaving in a docile manner. If taken from their mother at an early age, caracals can be easily tamed and leash-trained. When born they are the only cat that looks like a miniature version of their parents. In the wild they have been known to jump into a flock of birds, grabbing one with each paw and a third with the mouth. Their ear tufts are a definite aid in hearing, as determined by scientific tests in which the tufts have been cut off, causing the animal's hearing to be far less accurate.

Page 99
White Persian: *Felis Catus*

Comments: Persian cats, like Samoyed dogs, are believed to have descended from the steppe cats of central Asia. They supposedly have long fur and small ears, like Samoyeds, to protect them from the cold.

Ever since the domestication of cats they have been linked with female beauty. In ancient Rome the cat was associated with Venus, not only because of its amatory nature, but because it had long been identified with goddesses, among them Isis, Bast, Artemis, and Freyja.

Page 100
Ocelot: *Felis Pardalis*

Characteristics: weight twelve to thirty pounds; head and body length about thirty-five inches; tail about sixteen inches

Habitat: dense humid jungle to thorny chaparral; any sort of cover but rarely in the open

Habits: primarily nocturnal; extremely territorial; generally a ground hunter but does rest in trees during the day

Prey: birds, small deer, peccaries, monkeys, coatimundis, agoutis

Distribution: southern United States to South and Central America

Comments: PA: For years they were very popular as pets in this country, imported from South

America and sold in pet stores for as little as fifty dollars. Ocelot clubs were formed in many states to allow owners of these exotic cats to get together and compare notes on the breed. The most popular of these was the Long Island Ocelot Club, which still exists today. Ocelot populations in the wild and in captivity have decreased to the point that the cats are now on the endangered list. Their urine has a very offensive, pungent odor. Generally tend to be very mouthy cats, wanting to suck on fingers and failing that, to suck their own tails (in captivity).

Page 103
Himalayan Cat and Elephant: *Felis Catus*

Comments: The Himalayan today is the fastest-growing breed in the world. It is a hybrid that combines Persian conformation and coat quality with Siamese colors and patterns. An ancient Buddhist belief states that when an advanced person dies, his soul enters into the body of a cat, remaining there until the cat dies, upon which it enters heaven.

Mark Twain loved cats, and while traveling in Europe came across one that had an extraordinary relationship with an elephant: "In the Zoological Garden (of Marseille) we found specimens of all the animals the world produces, I think. . . . The boon companion of the colossal elephant was a common cat! This cat had a fashion of climbing up the elephant's hind legs, and roosting on his back.

She would sit up there, with her paws curved under breast, and sleep in the sun half the afternoon. It would annoy the elephant at first and he would reach up and take her down, but she would go aft and climb up again. She persisted and finally conquered the elephant's prejudices, and now they are inseparable friends. The cat plays about her comrade's forefeet or his trunk often, until dogs approach and then she goes aloft out of danger. The elephant has annihilated several dogs lately that pressed his companion too closely."

Page 105
African Lion Cub: *Panthera Leo*

Comments: Lion cub and Basenji dog both wear hunting bells around their necks. The Basenji, which is barkless, is the most catlike of all dogs, and African hunters attach bells to the dogs in order to follow them through the forest of marshes. A hand-raised cub, like this lion, particularly one that has been taken from its mother before its eyes have opened, will imprint or bond to the person caring for it and can, depending on the particular breed and the capacity of the person in charge, become very tame. As such an animal matures, it will treat the human as one of its own kind, playing and greeting the person by butting heads. A hand-raised lion, bobcat, or ocelot will generally become much more dependent and demanding of the love and affection of humans than will a domestic cat.

Page 106

Tortoiseshell Oriental Shorthair: *Felis Catus*

Comments: The tortoiseshell cat has a coat standard requirement of three colors—black, light red, and dark red. Its origins are obscure and it is virtually a female-only breed; males are extremely rare and invariably sterile.

When cats crossed over from Egypt to the Arabian countries of Islam, they found a rival revered animal in the horse. However, the popularity of the cat grew to match, if not surpass, that of Arabian equines. Even Mohammed owned a cat, a female called Muezza. Legend tells us that one afternoon Muezza was sleeping, cuddled up next to the prophet, who, having to get up but not wanting to disturb the sleep of his beloved pet, chose to cut off the sleeve of his robe on which the cat was sleeping. When the cat finally awakened and arched its back to show appreciation for the prophet's thoughtfulness, Mohammed blessed the cat by passing his hand over her back three times, thus granting her perpetual immunity from the danger of falling and ensuring cats a permanent place in Islamic paradise. From that moment on, the cat was blessed with the ability to land on its feet.

A Moslem riddle: Why do cats drink milk with their eyes closed? Answer: So that when Allah asks if they've had their milk, they can (with the hope of being given more) truthfully say they haven't seen any.

Even today, cats (but not dogs) are allowed inside mosques, where they are expected to control rat and mouse populations. In Islam cats are thought to be clean, dogs unclean.

Pages 108 and 109

Bobcat: *Felis Rufus*

Characteristics: weight fifteen to thirty-five pounds; head and body length about thirty inches; tail about six inches

Habitat: semidesert, subtropical swamp, forest, open rocky terrain

Habits: primarily nocturnal

Prey: squirrels, rabbits, other small mammals, birds, deer in winter, some domestic animals

Distribution: British Columbia and south and east to Central America

Comments: PA: Whereas in the wild, male felines will kill their offspring and other kittens they might happen upon, in captivity many males will frequently not only not harm their young but help with their rearing. Our male bobcat lies outside the den box while the female gives birth, then, when the kittens are at the age of about two weeks and begin coming out of the box, he gently plays and "talks" with them. Because bobcats like high vantage points, they often perch on the shoulders of their human companions. In their natural environment they have earned the name "wildcat" and are considered to be pound for pound the toughest feline in the wild. Hunters and naturalists claim to have never seen a frightened bobcat. Easily tamed in captivity if taken from their mother before their eyes have opened.

Pages 110 and 111
Sphynx: *Felis Catus*

Comments: The Sphynx, more than any other cat, perhaps, recalls the cats of Egypt and Rome. This is because practically the only reminders we have of those ancient felines are archaeological figures in bronze and metal that are also hairless and, unlike paintings, more reveal the cat's musculature, which causes it to appear more sinister and mysterious.

Practically from the beginning of his association with man, the cat has been linked with the occult. New York practicing witch Marion Weinstein tells us: "In witchcraft, and in other positive occult work, animal life is appreciated as all nature is revered. Witches and other positive magicians and sorcerers frequently keep many animals in their homes and communicate with others in the wild. . . . It's not only a popular tradition, it's a popular fact: cats and witches are compatible. . . . Even the predatory nature of cats is considered helpful to witches. It serves as a constant reminder of the dark side of the human and animal spirit, of the workings of life, death and rebirth on this planet. And this predatory instinct can be kept remarkably under control if the cat chooses to do so. The cat has often served in the role of the witch's familiar. A familiar is a nonhuman creature that helps the witch in most magic and occult work. The role of familiar goes far beyond the role of pet animal, because the familiar is both helper and companion to the witch; it is considered an equal."

Pages 112 and 113
Serval Kittens: *Felis Serval*

Comments: PA: As kittens servals are, perhaps, the most mellow of the exotic cats. However, as with most wild cats, at the age of a year and a half, with sexual maturity, they develop a mind of their own. Adult servals are generally not as tractable as caracals, lynxes, and bobcats. They use threat displays of much hissing, posturing, and paw striking—to impress and bluff. Trainers who work cats in shows generally replace animals once they become mature and more difficult, substituting younger cats. The older animals are then usually used as breeders.

Page 115
Calico Cat: *Felis Catus*

Comments: Calico cats come in both long-and short-haired varieties. The calico shorthair is believed to have originated in Spain, and is one of the earliest-known varieties. The calico is a difficult cat to reproduce since it is an almost all-female type. Colette, the famous author of *Gigi* and the Claudine novels, loved calicos and all cats; they figure in many of her books. Leonore Fleischer tells us that when Colette visited New York, with the usual celebrity hustle and bustle claiming her time and energies, she was returning to her Manhattan hotel one evening and spied a cat sitting in the street. At once she went over to talk to it, and the two of them mewed at each other for a friendly moment before Colette turned to her companion and said, with a heartfelt smile, *"Enfin! Quelqu'un qui parle français!"* ("Finally! Someone who speaks French!")

Page 117
Abyssinian: *Felis Catus*

Comments: Young Abyssinian pictured with a Basenji puppy. Dogs and cats possess the ability to be friends if given the chance, and in ancient Egypt Basenji and Abyssinian were supposedly common house pets. Apart from not barking, although it is not silent, the Basenji has no body odor, licks itself continually like a cat to keep clean, uses its paws as much or more than its mouth in play, loves to curl up on its owner's chest or lap, does not like water, and frequently arches its body when stretching. It is also often standoffish with strangers but entirely devoted to its owner.

Page 118
Silver Persian: *Felis Catus*

Comments: Long-haired cats generally believed to be the descendants of animals brought to Europe in the sixteenth century from Persia or Turkey. The cats' belle époque in Europe was during the Victorian period. It has been written that "partly it was the spirit of the age itself, an age of gingerbread artifice and sentiment, which led to this ascendancy. In this decorous and decorative epoch, there was a new awareness of the rich variety and stylish grace and beauty of the cat, a heightened appreciation of the creature as a domestic *objet d'art*. Venerated as a guardian of the home, honored as a mouser, the cat was now celebrated as a thing of beauty. In 1871 the first cat show was organized by Harrison Weir in London's Crystal Palace."

We are told that "during the eighteenth and early nineteenth centuries, the cat became the darling of the beau monde of the French bourgeoisie. Mme. de Staël, Mme. Récamier and the Duchess de

Bouillon were all cat fanciers, and Mme. Helvétius decked out her cats like fine ladies, swaddling them in fur robes and silk costumes."

Page 120
Puma: *Felis Concolor*

Characteristics: weight about one hundred to two hundred pounds; head and body about forty-six to sixty inches; tail about twenty-eight inches

Habitat: variable, from coniferous forest to desert

Habits: primarily diurnal; solitary and territorial over wide range

Prey: deer, wild sheep and goats, peccaries, beavers, ground birds, various small mammals, fish, large insects, and occasionally domestic animals

Distribution: North and South America

Comments: Also known as cougars, catamounts, painters, and mountain lions. Pumas are often said to kill for the love of killing, a reputation that has its source in those instances when a cat will kill several sheep or more in an enclosure. What probably really does happen is that in the case of deer and other wild prey, the puma will go after one victim, and once he has downed it and the other animals have escaped, he then calmly eats his meal. Whereas when a cougar is confronted with a herd of sheep, he kills one only to find himself surrounded by other panicky prey, still in close range. His hunting instincts propel him to keep killing until there are no more prey to stimulate his inner mechanism for attacking that which is food to him and is still alive and near and trying to escape.

PA: One of our first experiences with exotic cats was seeing an adult cougar, leopard, and tiger in the same cage with a Saint Bernard dog. They had been raised together and lived together as the best of friends. This often happens in captivity with hand-raised cats who would not normally frequent the same wild habitat. Chirpa, our cougar, and Scruffy, the bobcat, were raised together and were very attached to one another. They still talk to one another from their cages, but we no longer allow them to get together, since the difference in their sizes and strength could make for a dangerous situation if their play became too rough. During kitten season I often house baby servals, caracals, and bobcats together.

Page 122
Brown-and-White Tabby Shorthair: *Felis Catus*

Comments: In eighteenth- and nineteenth-century Europe, cat owners often had their portraits painted with their pets. Painters and sculptors who included cats in their work: Leonardo da Vinci, Ingres, Manet, Picasso, Renoir, Gauguin, Delacroix, Géricault, and Hogarth. Some of these animals were depicted rubbing against their owner in that familiar cat habit. Cats have scent glands on their heads and faces. When we stroke their heads, the gland leaves a faint scent of them on our hands, and the cat enjoys the odor as much as the stroking. For this same reason, they bump heads in signs of affection, and this is why they "nose-kiss" other cats.

Page 125
African lion: *Panthera Leo*

Comments: PA: No matter how "tame" a hand-raised wild cat appears, it is still a wild animal and will always possess this basic instinct. For this reason the persons who interact with such cats must continually be alert for signs of uneasiness or danger. All wild felines in domestic situations possess the ability to seriously injure or—in the case of the larger animals—kill the humans with whom they associate. In most cases a cat will give some sort of warning, which the person must be aware enough of feline behavior to detect. Humans working with wild cats must continually maintain both caution and a respect for the cat's potential danger. However, tame felines released to the wild will often continue to be affectionate with their former human companions. George Adamson's lions that were hand-raised and released in the wild still venture into his camp to butt heads with him and then leave. Joy Adamson's Elsa returned to camp from the wild, bringing with her her cubs for Joy to

admire and share, allowing them to be touched and observed. A family in Arizona hand-raised two bobcat kittens that had been orphaned in the wild, allowing them to live inside their house and play and sleep with their young children. As the cats grew older they were allowed to live freely outside but to come and go as they chose. However, they did periodically return to the family, affectionate and tame, before going off to hunt and roam again.

Page 127
Cream Shorthair: *Felis Catus*

Comments: Cats seem to love the scent of certain plants and flowers, among them lavender, leeks, eucalyptus, carnations, papyrus, asparagus, mint, catnip, oleander (dangerous), valerian, mimosa, and cat thyme. Apart from oleander, plants that are poisonous or dangerous to cats are lily of the valley, lantana, poinsettia, azalea, hydrangea, elephant-ear, and mistletoe.

The composure of this cat could in seconds be radically changed if he were introduced to that delight of all felines—catnip. Vicky McMillan tells us: "Give a typical cat catnip, and he will show a striking change in behavior—vigorously purring, growling, rolling, leaping into the air. These are all common feline reactions to *Nepeta cataria*, a species of plant strangely attractive to cats. Furthermore, not only domestic types exhibit this behavior; lions and other wild members of the cat family also enjoy catnip, and lynxes have even been trapped using oil of catnip as bait. Individual reactions to catnip vary, of course, some cats showing greater interest than others.

"What makes cats behave so strangely around catnip? So far, no one understands the phenomenon in detail. It is known that, while their sense of smell is not as acute as some other senses, cats do react strongly to the odor of catnip; it is this odor, apparently, rather than the eating of catnip leaves, that produces the typical ecstatic resonse. To some extent, catnip seems to function as a tranquilizer. Catnip is also regarded as a cat aphrodisiac, and the rolling response is remarkably similar to the behavior of a female in heat. Some cat experts advise giving catnip to prospective mates to promote successful pairing, particularly if one or both cats are inexperienced.

"Catnip is a member of the mint family and related to such kitchen herbs as sage and thyme. Originally from Europe, it was introduced in America long ago as a common plant in herb gardens. It soon escaped cultivation and now grows wild around old homesteads and farms. Reaching a height of about three feet, catnip has heart-shaped leaves that are toothed around their edges, and small white or pinkish spotted flowers. It blooms between July and September."

ACKNOWLEDGMENTS

This book could never have been started or finished had it not been for the time and help that were generously given by a number of people, some from different countries, some who speak different languages—but animal lovers all.

First I would like to thank Bill and Penny Andrews for their continued support and hospitality. Friends who also contributed hours, days, and expertise on numerous occasions were: Layna Lundgren, Clark Miers, Ron Henriques, Cheri Wilkerson, David York, Rich Messena, Ron and Roxann Whitfield, and Caroline Osier.

The San Diego Zoo and the San Diego Wild Animal Park were, from beginning to end, supportive of this book, as they have been in the past. Of the many fine and talented people who helped me there I would especially like to thank Georgeanne Irvine, Kathy Marmack, Heidi Enslew, Alison Wood, Amy Wing, Carlee Robinson, Terry Willingham, Boo Shaw, JoAnn Thomas, Chris Peterson, Jeff Fuller, Alan Roocroft, and Pat Humphry.

At Marine World—Africa USA, I would like to thank Mark Jardarian, Lori Collard, Jeff Gloss, Pat Martin-Vegue, Steve Castillo, Jamie Uyehara, and Cecelia Pleshakou.

Special gratitude I also express to my friend Lee Keaton, who lived for animals and also died for them.

For their interest and help I also thank good friends John and Bo Derek, as well as Duane Pillsbury and his wife, Joan Embery.

Other persons who made generous contributions were those magical and legendary gentlemen Siegfried and Roy, as well as David Maré, Seymour Heller, Carol Berkowitz, Gale Koos, Ron and Donna Lemelin, Tim and Bev Bailey, Lora Vigne, José Redondo, Charles Bowen, Lynn Dougherty and the Old Globe Theatre of San Diego, Tracy King, Dick Broün and Sheril Lisonbee, Esther McKelvey, C. C. and Barbara Mendenhall, Kitty Whitwier, Pam Rogers, Anita Sentovic, Darlene LaMadrid, Bradley Smith, Tracy Askew, Jack Fitzgerald, Joan Benson, Linda Lewis and *Cat Fancy* magazine, and Pam Bates and Friends of Cats of El Cajon.

I am deeply and especially grateful to my mother and to my brother, Ron, and sister-in-law, Gale, for taking care of me during most of this book; to José Franco for his help with the European side of this effort; to Gale Cooper for sound advice and enthusiasm; to Twyla Cecile for her ideas; to Mesa Photo and Chromacolor for their work with my film; to Rick Fabares for all of his time and creative effort; to Barbara Chance (who did the superb drawing for my unicorn book) for her help in designing this one; to Joe Saccoman, my friend, who accompanied me on many shoots and contributed to their successes; to Patty and Bill Saccoman for providing me with transportation; to José Lopez for keeping my cameras working; to Nancy Ridley for typing manuscript; to Barbara Cox for her good advice; and to Elias Garcia and his staff for the color separations.

For believing in this project from its conception I thank my agent, Gloria Loomis, my European associate, Rudolf Blanckenstein, and at William Morrow, my editor, Joan Nagy, as well as Howard Cady, Lawrence Hughes, Sherry Arden, Al Marchioni, and Lela Rolontz.

Tiger footprint